cracked
linda tubby

Creative and Easy Ways to Cook Eggs

Photography by Ali Allen

KYLE BOOKS

I dedicate *Cracked* to my sons Dan and Ben,
partners Ellie and Angie

&

my sister Carole, the hen lover of the family,
who would sing to our hens as a child
with love

Huge thanks must go to Lucy Gavaghan who so effectively campaigns to
have caged hens' eggs removed from sale in the UK's major supermarkets

Over 1,000 good eggs were cracked during the
making of this book!
So my thanks to the good hens that laid them

First published in Great Britain in 2017 by
Kyle Books, an imprint of Kyle Cathie Ltd.
192–198 Vauxhall Bridge Road
London SW1V 1DX
general.enquiries@kylebooks.com
www.kylebooks.co.uk

10 9 8 7 6 5 4 3 2 1

ISBN 978 0 85783 388 4

Text © 2017 Linda Tubby
Design © 2017 Kyle Books
Photography © 2017 Ali Allen

Designer: nic&lou
Photographer: Ali Allen
Food Stylist: Linda Tubby
Prop Stylist: Iris Bromet
Project Editor: Sophie Allen
Copy Editor: Stephanie Evans
Editorial Assistant: Hannah Coughlin
Production: Nic Jones, Gemma John and Lisa Pinnell

A Cataloguing in Publication record for this title is
available from the British Library.

Colour reproduction by ALTA London
Printed in China by 1010 International Printing Ltd.

Please be careful serving raw or lightly cooked eggs to
the young, elderly or pregnant as there may be a risk of
food-borne illness.

Contents

Introduction

The aim of this book is to have everyone's favourite egg recipes in one basket. Some classics, tried and tested for family gatherings, plus lots of easy, innovative eggy ideas for tasty everyday meals and a guide to simple egg cookery. With, of course, loads of delicious and unmissable indulgences.

The recipes cover the simplest dishes with easy-to-find and readily available ingredients. The humble egg gives such culinary freedom, a perfectly packaged source of protein that can be whipped up in so many meals. It is also, compared to meat and fish, one that is fantastically cheap, so it's worth adding a little extra to your egg budget and taking personal responsibility to buy the very best eggs you can find.

An egg given with love in any cooked form for anyone makes a comforting offering whatever the occasion. Whether providing the ideal start to a busy day, a leisurely brunch for a small gathering, a creamy dessert or comforting supper dish, eggs will always find an appreciative audience.

Egg potential

The egg is just an egg until put in the hands of a creative cook. Then with sublime alchemy it can be transformed into so many wonderful dishes. This superstar of the kitchen can be swiftly turned into quick, satisfying meals with economy or extravagance. Nutritious meals are a breeze with eggs as your ally.

Eggs aren't just for breakfast, so break out of the box and give them full daytime status too. You won't go hungry with a dozen eggs in the kitchen. How else would we toss together those Sunday breakfast pancakes or a huge brunch omelette? Enjoy high-rise soufflés, whip up blousy meringues, emulsify sunset-yellow mayonnaise or even clarify a bone broth to a crystal-clear consommé? We create velvety custards as the base for delicious ice creams and nursery puddings; we savour a scramble and perfect a poached egg – comfort food at its simplest and very best.
So let's get cracking!

What's in an egg?

Eggs in whatever form are entirely natural and nutritionally dense, packed with high-quality protein and nutrients, vitamins, minerals, antioxidants and lipids, all of which aid muscle strength, as well as heart, brain and eye function, and combat disease. A hen egg averages about 70 calories, which means including them in your diet is also great for weight management. Start the day with a boiled, poached or scrambled egg or a simple folded omelette and you won't feel the need for more food as quickly. Try adding a sprinkling of crushed nuts, a little extra virgin olive oil and some watercress leaves for a super-satisfying breakfast.

Scrambling, poaching or omelette-making shouldn't send the cook into a panic – eggs are so forgiving and, after all, it's a question of personal taste rather than right or wrong. My golden rule when cooking eggs (or for that matter any kind of cooking) is to be in the moment, enjoy doing your best and most of all have fun experimenting.

Crack the egg at its widest point on the side of the carrier bowl with two sharp taps and, using both thumbs, ease the shell in two. Let some white slip into the carrier bowl, then gently tip the yolk from one half shell to the other until all the white has flopped into the bowl. Tip the yolk into its bowl and the white into the other and repeat the process. If at any point very tiny bits of shell or spots of yolk get into the whites, scoop them out using one side of the rounded shell; it acts like a magnet. If you end up with a lot of broken yolk and a messed-up white you have only wasted one egg. Tip that into a cup, beat with a fork and keep in the fridge to use within a day – you can add it to a light mayonnaise (see page 14) a scramble or an omelette. Start again with a clean carrier bowl.

- **_Saving spare yolks and whites_**

Where a recipe calls for either the yolks or the whites, whichever you don't need immediately can be kept for a different dish. Whole yolks can be carefully covered – so they don't break – by a little water and a lid and stored in the fridge for two days. The whites can be put in a screw-topped jar, labelled to remind you how many there are, and kept in the fridge for up to a week. If you have a lot of either yolks or whites, freeze them:

For every 6 yolks mix together with ½ teaspoon of either salt or sugar, tip into a suitable container, labelling it to indicate the number of yolks and whether they are for savoury or sweet use, and freeze for up to 2 months. The whites simply freeze without mixing with salt or sugar. They will keep frozen for up to 3 months and I find they whisk well after freezing and thawing. Remember to defrost them in the fridge.

Check the expiry dates on stored eggs regularly. If you have more than you can use before their 'best before' date, separate the whites from the yolks and freeze them to use for meringues and baking. Or whisk up the whole eggs, label to indicate the quantity and freeze to use within a month for baking only.

Know your eggs

Easy egg separation

The confident cook needs to crack this painless aspect of egg cookery and discover why it's so useful. Getting your eggs separated cleanly without any trace of yolk in the whites is what you need, as a tiny scrap will inhibit the volume egg white foam can achieve. The main aim is to keep the egg yolk whole, the white free from yolk and both free from bits of shell. Here's how: Have two bowls at the ready in sizes you need for the recipe plus a small carrier bowl to hold and transfer one white at a time.

Good egg ... bad egg ...

To gauge the freshness of your eggs, fill a deep clear glass bowl with cold water up to a level about 2½ times the height of the egg. Gently lower the egg into the water. A very fresh egg will immediately sink to the bottom and lie flat horizontally. This is because the air pocket within the egg is very small. Use these eggs for poaching, scrambling and frying or for making ice creams and custards.

A slightly older egg will still lie on the bottom of the bowl but at a very slight angle, the round end uppermost. Good for boiling as they peel easily and also use for omelettes and baking.

As the egg starts to lose its freshness it will dry out, the air pocket gets larger and the egg will begin to bob almost upright. The pointed end will still lie on the bottom of the bowl, while the rounder end (where the air pocket is) will point towards the surface. However, the egg will still be good enough for baking and meringues.

It's very important once this test is done to use the egg right away for cooking, as the shell will now be porous and the egg will start to deteriorate.

If the egg leaves the bottom of the bowl and floats completely on the surface of the water, it should be thrown out, as it will most certainly be too bad even for baked cakes.

The versatile egg

How do you like your eggs in the morning? Move over granola and welcome the egg for breakfast. The first meal of the day is so important for energy, and what better way to show affection than to prepare a perfectly soft-boiled egg for loved ones to enjoy? It takes no time to cook, served up really hot with thickly buttered toasted soldiers to dip comfortingly into the runny yolk. Eggs, the number-one comfort food, can make us feel cosseted. Even if you do this once a week for someone or, just as important, for yourself, you will feel the rich benefits of one of the healthiest and cheapest forms of protein.

- *Soft boiled*
3–4 minutes will give a softish white and a runny yolk.

The term 'boiled' is a bit of a contradiction as that's the last thing you want to put your egg through. A simmered egg would be more to the point so it doesn't crash around the pan and crack. Also, it's best to select a pan that allows eggs to sit in a single layer.

First get everything in place. It's easier and quicker to boil a large kettle of water for your egg pan as well as for a pot of tea or coffee – it's infinitely faster. Prepare

your plate with freshly buttered toast cut into soldiers, freshly ground pepper and crunchy salt crystals.

Pour boiling water from the kettle into a pan, bring back to the boil and lower the heat so the water isn't moving. Gently add the eggs and leave for 30 seconds (this stops them cracking from shock), then increase the heat to a simmer and time your eggs to perfection.

For real satisfaction, a runny yolk is what's needed with the white just set. If you cut off the top and the white looks a little loose simply pop the top back on, read a few paragraphs from the morning paper, have a swig of tea and all will be well: your egg will be perfect in no time, cooked by residual heat. This is a good reason not to crack the top of your egg with the back of the spoon.

As well as being ideal for breakfast, a soft-boiled egg can comfort after an evening out if you didn't manage supper. It's the easiest and most satisfying filler when you come home tired and starving. As in all things there's more than one way to boil the perfect egg. You could put your egg into cold water and, once the water boils, turn to a simmer and time the process to get the kind of softness you want from your egg. This method can work but you need to watch the pan constantly.

- *Mollet, soft in the centre, yet easy to peel*
**5–6 minutes will give a slightly firmer white –
enough so the egg can be peeled easily even
though the yolk is hot and very soft.**

This method is a good substitute for poached eggs and also served hot. Slightly older eggs are better when you intend to boil then peel them as they peel more easily when 5 or so days old. Pour boiling water from the kettle into a pan, bring back to the boil then lower the heat. Carefully add the eggs to prevent them cracking from shock, then increase the heat to a simmer and time your eggs to perfection. Plunge the eggs straight into cold water to stop them cooking instantly. Gently crack the shell and carefully peel right away while still hot inside but just cool enough to handle. Put into warm water as you continue to peel the rest if you want to eat them hot; otherwise put into cold water and reheat later.

- *Hard boiled*
**7–9 minutes will give varying degrees of
firmness to the yolk.**

A thin, greenish-grey film may form around the yolk. This harmless discoloration is simply a visual indicator of a natural chemical reaction. Sulphur from the amino acids in the white of the egg is reacting with iron in the yolk, causing a film of iron sulphide to form on the yolk's surface. Heat speeds up this discoloration: so the longer your eggs boil, the darker it becomes so don't overcook them. Plunging the eggs straight into cold water helps to prevent the ring forming. Then crack and peel right away from the rounded end – even if still warm this makes it easier. Then put them into fresh water straight away to cool down.

• *Boiling tips*

Just before boiling you could shallowly (just to pierce the shell, no further) prick the rounded end of the eggshell with the tip of a clean pin. This releases the pressure from the air pocket and so stops the egg bursting on contact with the hot water. Try gently stirring your simmering eggs: this action is said to centralise the yolk – useful in a recipe that calls for the eggs to be cut in half such as Devilled eggs (page 128).

• *The fine art of poaching*

There is poached and poached, the one where the yellow yolk shines through a white veil, and the one that looks like a compact, oval, wrapped silk parcel with the yolk hidden in the middle.

We all have pretensions toward the latter, as it looks cheffy and professional, but the reality is a more homely look is much nicer as it doesn't involve a lot of vinegar. Restaurants often use up to 3 tablespoons for 4 eggs to help coagulate the white. This trend was introduced by the famous Mrs Beeton in 1861, so she is to blame! Fresh eggs don't need lots of vinegar to be poached perfectly. I think vinegar flavours the egg white too much, but do try a little if you want to experiment – it does work. Never, though, add salt to the water as it breaks down the egg white.

In a fresh egg, the white will be much tighter. Cloudy whites can indicate very fresh eggs straight after lay, so don't be put off but, for poaching, eggs around three days old are best. The very thick white will naturally

form a good oval shape, encasing the yolk as it hits the water. With slightly older eggs the thinning white floats off in the water and you don't get such a compact rounded poach. It's not a disaster and is perfectly acceptable, as it will still taste good and the loose bits can be trimmed away.

If cooking eggs individually for a few people, or just one for yourself, crack the egg into a small glass and create a whirlpool in the pan by stirring the boiling water, then plop the egg into the middle, turn down the heat and time it for 3 minutes. If you can't lower the heat enough, turn it off and let the egg poach for up to a minute longer, or until the white feels firm and the yolk is soft but cooked. Gently scoop the egg out of the pan with a slotted spoon, resting the spoon briefly on kitchen paper to absorb the drips, then put it straight onto your plate.

If you are poaching eggs this way for a few people and want everyone to eat together, scoop them straight into cold water. To reheat them all at once put them in a bowl of just-boiled water for around 2 minutes. They will last in cold water in the fridge for up to two days, ready to reheat when needed.

If you have super-fresh eggs and feel like poaching a few at the same time, a shallower sauté-style pan is good to use. Fill it with around 7cm of just-boiled water from the kettle. Crack one egg at a time straight into the water. To do this, get the water simmering then crack the egg by giving it two sharp taps on the side of a bowl set close to the pan. Gently lift to the surface of the water and separate the shells, letting the egg plop in. When all the eggs are in the pan turn the heat down so the water is barely moving and time them for 3 minutes or turn off the heat and allow up to a minute

longer. Lift out each one with a slotted spoon, resting the base of the spoon on kitchen paper to absorb the drips, then quickly place onto the serving plates.

There is another method that works with slightly older eggs where, before cracking, you give the egg a dip in barely moving water. This sets the thinnest outer part of the white onto the shell, so as the eggs are cracked open you are left with the thickest part of the white, which will then wrap itself around the yolk when it hits the water. If trying out this trick, get two pans of simmering water at the ready. Dip the egg, still in its shell, into one pan for 30 seconds. Lift out with a slotted spoon into cold water to cool, just enough to be able to handle it. Crack the egg open into a small glass and do the poaching in the second pan of clean water as above. This avoids dirty water.

• *Let's scramble*

Eggs are mostly uncomplicated in the area of one-pan cookery and amazingly satisfying. For me, scrambled egg is the most comforting of all popular basic egg dishes – it's my number one. It's so easy to transform a simple scramble into something special and very tasty. Put some herbs and chilli into a freshly made scramble and serve with a sharp tomato and finely chopped onion salsa. That's not to forget the classic, an easy scramble with sliced smoked salmon folded in and plenty of freshly ground black pepper... is there anything better?

The two best ways to crack the case:
There's no doubt that whichever method you choose, good scrambled eggs are quick and simple to knock up, taking only around 3 minutes to achieve. Patience is key: being in the moment and stirring over a low heat is crucial. Allow 2 eggs per person.

Crack the eggs into a bowl just prior to cooking, breaking them up lightly with a fork – there should be no furious whisking involved. I like to add half an eggshell of water for every 3 eggs, as this lightens the scramble, but some like to add milk, cream or extra butter, making a slightly heavier, creamier finish. You can add one or two extra yolks to the whole eggs for richness, or add another egg white to the mixture to make them lighter. I add salt once the eggs are cooked, as it tends to toughen the mixture if added earlier. I also prefer to add freshly ground black or white pepper at the table.

Have everything you intend to accompany your scramble ready to roll, including just warmed plates.

For 4 eggs, melt about 15g butter, clarified butter, ghee or oil if you wish, in a preheated – preferably nonstick

– medium pan over a low heat. Without letting the butter fizz, pour in the eggs and stir constantly with a wooden spoon, the perfect implement whichever way you choose to scramble. As the eggs start to cook on the base of the pan you may find they have a firm, curd-like texture in parts. If this happens, the protein is hardening too fast, so you need to get the heat lower, or it's often easier to keep moving the pan off and on the heat. Stir the slightly firmer, wavy curds into the still-soft mixture, and keep stirring until it comes together in a loose yet cooked mass with a little texture to it; this takes no more than 1½ minutes. Mix in a pinch or so of sea salt crystals once the eggs are cooked (if you are folding smoked salmon through the soft scramble, you may not need salt at all).

The second method, for a very soft and creamy-looking scramble with a uniform loose texture, involves the bain-marie. Set a bowl over a pan of barely simmering water – about 3cm will get enough steam circulating. Use a bowl large enough so it doesn't touch the water. (You could use a double boiler if you possess such a thing.) Stir the eggs with a knob of butter in the usual way to a thickened creamy mass. This method may take longer, around 6 minutes of continuous stirring, but it is a reliable way to achieve this softer scramble.

Whichever method you go for, remember the scramble will continue to cook away from the heat, so remove it when it's a little wetter than you want. When it's cooked to your liking, serve quickly while very hot and oh so comforting. If a scramble overcooks, quickly add a few tablespoons of thick cream.

- ### *Fried softly softly or crispy and golden*

A fried egg is a very personal thing. Some like a soft white edge just set with a glassy yellow yolk and others prefer a crisply, fried golden frilly edge with a pale veil covering the soft yolk. Then there are all the variations in between as well as options to flip over.

- ### *To shallow fry*

Heat good dripping, raw coconut oil, rapeseed oil, olive oil, butter, clarified butter or ghee in a frying pan. You can cook 3 or 4 eggs at a time in a frying pan with a 20–22cm base, or use a smaller pan to cook just one. Crack in the eggs and let them set for a minute tilting the pan and spooning the oil over the egg. Then decide to serve as it just sets or carry on frying until crispy around the edges and the yolk is anything from still soft and yellow or with a pale veil. At any point you can cover the pan to ensure the yolk sets to your liking.

If you want to go 'over easy', flip the cooked egg over with a spatula once the white has set. Carry on cooking to set the yolk to your liking, the aim being not to break the yolk although some people quite like a firmer or even a broken yolk.

- ### *To deep-fry*

Heat 1cm rapeseed oil, olive oil, raw coconut oil or ghee in a wok or high-sided pan until hot. A good test is to drop in a cube of bread: if it sizzles and turns golden straight away, the oil is hot enough (adjust the heat up or down as needed). Crack an egg into a small glass, then carefully tip into the oil. Immediately bring the white part over the yolk using two spoons so the yolk doesn't overcook.

• *The comforting omelette*

'You can't make a good omelette if you put too much butter in the frying pan ... It's not difficult to make an omelette but it's quite hard to describe exactly how it should be made without making it sound very difficult indeed.'

These pearls of wisdom came from Marcel Boulestin in his book *Eggs – 120 ways of cooking eggs*, which he wrote in 1932. He had an exclusive restaurant in Covent Garden and was the first TV chef at the end of the 1930s. He was a great inspiration to Elizabeth David and he has also inspired me to write this book.

A simple folded **French omelette** needs a preheated hot pan so it cooks very quickly. The butter or any other good fat or oil should just fizz (not brown) before adding the lightly forked-over eggs – the more you beat the eggs for an omelette, the tougher it will be. Add the mixture to the pan and use the flat side of a fork, passing it under the eggs to keep them moving, until you have the set you want. Fold about a third of the omelette towards the middle, then fold the opposite third over the top, quickly shaking the pan until it falls on the plate beautifully soft and folded yet just firm and still pale yellow. If you want something firmer and golden, just cook for a little longer. To make a herby variation, see page 97.

If serving more than one person, making individual omelettes is best. They are so fast to make, it's always best to give a swift wipe of the pan before replenishing with more butter for the next omelette, vital for a fresh-tasting experience. A runny omelette will take 1 minute or less, firm 1½ minutes and well cooked around 2.

A **French omelette** is folded into a half moon or folded into three but never flipped right over to cook the other side. Often much softer in texture with the filling (if there is one) added before the omelette is folded to encase it rather than mixed into the raw eggs.

A **Tortilla** or **Spanish omelette** is cooked in a pan on one side, then inverted onto a plate and slid back into a wiped-out pan to cook on the other side (see page 105). It is often served cut into bite-size squares either warm or cold. The exception is the Majorcan tortilla (see page 90) which has whipped egg white added so needs a touch of the grill to burnish it golden.

The **Frittata**, or **Italian omelette**, is a combination of the two styles. Always leave the precooked filling ingredients to cool a little before mixing into the eggs in the bowl or the pan. Cook on one side until bubbles appear and the edges are just set, and then finish under a grill until puffed and golden (see pages 96 and 102).

No matter which part of the world the omelette is from, you can adapt the recipes in this book to use ingredients you instinctively like to put together to complement your eggs and, more encouragingly, have spare in the fridge, or can find in your local open-all-hours ethnic corner grocery shop on the way home. Be sensitive, though: you want to avoid conflicting flavours by overloading your omelette simply because you have things that need using up.

• *Soothing baked eggs*

The French brasserie favourite *oeufs en cocotte*, where the eggs are simply baked in cream, can be as simple or as fancy as you like (see page 146). These are sometimes called shirred eggs. Cracked into ramekins, the eggs can be placed in a roasting tin filled up to the middle of the dishes with barely simmering water and

cooked in the oven covered with foil. Alternatively, use a large, deep-sided frying pan on the hob and cover with a lid. Baked eggs can also be cooked in individual gratin dishes in the oven without the need for water. It's much easier, though, cooking *en cocotte,* as below.

Begin by preheating the oven to 190°C/gas mark 5 and liberally buttering as many shallow ramekins as you need. Scatter in freshly ground black or white pepper and sea salt crystals. Crack an egg or two into each ramekin and spoon over 1–2 tablespoons double cream, crème fraîche or soured cream, avoiding the yolk. Sit the ramekins in a tin filled with hot water as described above, cover and bake for about 6 minutes. Check the whites are fully set and the yolks cooked to your liking. They keep on cooking from the heat of the dish for a few minutes, then they are ready to serve with thickly buttered toast.

•   *Marvellous meringues*

Given time, excess energy, a strong arm and the right level of commitment, it is perfectly possible – in fact highly desirable and rewarding – to experience at least once in life making the perfect meringue using nothing more than a balloon whisk. But if you prefer an easier life you are much better off using an efficient hand-held electric beater – an implement most cooks possess. Using this method you have something to be proud of within minutes.

Spanking-clean, by which I mean totally grease-free, equipment is the next step to success. Nothing should be allowed to interfere with the ability egg whites have to form bubbles, so grease is the enemy here, not the cook in charge. Plastic bowls are never good to use: it seems egg white and plastic just don't have the right chemistry. The idea is gradually to get as much air into

the whites as possible so they increase in volume by up to eight times, so use a good-sized glass, china or stainless-steel bowl.

If you are using stored whites from the fridge for your meringues, put them in the bowl and cover for around 30 minutes before whisking. If they are stored frozen, defrost in the fridge overnight, then follow the instructions above.

With what seems like so many dos and don'ts, it's easy to think there is some mystery in the making of meringues, but it's simply a question of common sense and a touch of practice. Older egg whites are perfect for meringue as the albumen is thinner, but that means the yolks aren't so good to use for other dishes. So collect the whites left over from dishes involving fresher egg yolks only, and keep in a jar in the fridge for up to a week, or freeze them, but always remember to mark the container with how many whites there are.

• **French** or **simple meringue** is the most basic meringue and the most popular. It's certainly my favourite as it's quick and easy once the method is learnt. It has a light delicate texture perfect for any dessert. Sugar is whisked into the foamed whites in a ratio of 2 whites (2 fresh medium egg whites weigh 75g) to about 110g caster sugar. This will make about 6 blousy meringues. Once cooked and cooled, they will keep in an airtight container for two weeks.

A large pinch of cream of tartar added at the start prevents the foam from losing its shape if you overwhisk; salt doesn't have the same chemistry. Cream of tartar helps to stabilise the proteins as they become lighter and makes them easier to shape prior to adding the sugar. Adding the sugar then stabilises the foam further when it's whisked in gradually and continuously.

Once the whites are gradually whisked up to a firm peak stage the beaters leave a pattern in the foam as they rotate and you will be able to hold the bowl upside down without the mixture sliding down. Moisture isn't good for meringues, so never weigh out the sugar too soon as it attracts moisture from the air – open a fresh bag of sugar, or take the top off your airtight jar just before you whisk the whites.

At this stage you can start to shower in the sugar, a few tablespoons at a time, continuing to whisk as you add. The whisking helps to dissolve the sugar crystals, creating greater volume and a stiff glossy finish, so adding gradually is important. It also prevents the sugar bubbling out of the meringue as it cooks.

If the phone rings and you have to leave a made-up meringue, never rewhisk the stiffened mixture once the sugar has been added as the volume will diminish. Folding gently with a spatula will just about work, whisking not! Sugars that are dense, like coconut palm sugar and many unrefined sugars, tend to bring down the volume of the meringue after 5 or so tablespoons have been whisked in. So it's advisable to dry them in the oven and cool them before processing in a coffee grinder to make them as fine as possible and use them with a proportion of caster sugar to keep the mixture light.

• **Italian meringue** is made with hot sugar syrup using 165g caster sugar for every 3 whites, or for an even stiffer meringue use 190g sugar. Put the sugar in a pan with 3 tablespoons boiling water from the kettle. Place over a low heat and, once the sugar has dissolved to a very clear syrup, increase the heat and boil to a temperature of 121°C. If you have no thermometer, boil for 4 minutes, but watch it doesn't caramelise. Whisk the whites with a pinch of cream of tartar until the beaters leave a pattern in the foam as they rotate, then gradually pour in the syrup, whisking continuously. To speed up the cooling process put the bowl in a large basin of cold water and whisk until tepid. It's a good stable meringue for piping as a topping and browning under the grill or with a blowtorch. Try adding some to the lemon tartlets on page 180.

• **Swiss meringue** is often known as cooked meringue and is good for piped decorations and dessert bases. It has a harder, more dense texture than the other meringues. It's whisked as it heats over a bain-marie. The ratio here is again 2 whites to 110g caster sugar. Mix the whites and sugar in a bowl large enough to sit over a pan of barely simmering water so the base doesn't touch the water. Whisk until the temperature reaches 40°C, or if you haven't got a thermometer it will take 8 minutes for it to thicken so the beaters leave patterns in the mixture as they rotate. Remove from the heat. To speed up the cooling process, put the bowl in a large basin of cold water and whisk until tepid.

Needs and musts

The magic of eggs proves irresistible: they bind, blend and whisk. They really are the wonder ingredient, the cook's friend in the kitchen, so here are a few simple must-have extras.

• *Mastering the art of mayonnaise*

It still seems like alchemy that two basic ingredients like egg and oil can emulsify to make such an interesting complexity of flavours. Once you start making your own mayonnaise you won't want to revert to the bought version however good they are these days. Making your own, you know the source and quality of all the ingredients. It will keep for 4 days covered in the fridge.

Start with 3 egg yolks at room temperature. Whisk in 2 teaspoons Dijon mustard, 2 teaspoons white balsamic vinegar and a good pinch of sea salt flakes. Measure out 200ml sunflower oil and 100ml extra virgin olive oil or use 300ml rapeseed oil. Slowly at first drip in the oil – it's key to a good mayonnaise so that the oil droplets have a chance to break down and start emulsifying with the yolk. A squeezy plastic ketchup dispenser does this well, or once you're deft at this gradual process, drip it straight from the measuring jug used to measure the oil. Once the mixture starts to thicken you can then add the oil in a slow steady stream. To prevent the mixture splitting I like to add a drop or so of lemon juice after the first 50ml oil has been incorporated which helps to stabilise the emulsion. Taste and adjust the seasoning with more salt if needed.

If the mayonnaise splits, whisk in droplets of hot water and, once it comes together again, carry on adding the oil as before. Or mix a single egg yolk in a bowl and start continuously whisking in the split mixture again in droplets – this is an option that works well. This doesn't often happen but it's usually down to a loss of concentration.

Mayonnaise variations

- *Add 1 tablespoons wasabi paste instead of Dijon mustard.*
- *Use lime juice instead of lemon juice.*
- *Try English mustard instead of Dijon or 1 tablespoon horseradish instead of mustard, added at the end.*
- *Simmer the juice of 2 oranges until reduced down to a tablespoon and add to the mayonnaise half-way through.*
- *For an aioli, crush 3 fat cloves of garlic to a fine paste with some sea salt crystals and add with the mustard. Check the flavour at the end before adding any extra salt.*
- *To make a light mayonnaise use 2 whole eggs and 300ml sunflower oil and combine in a blender with the other ingredients.*

Simple vanilla custard

Heat 150ml double cream and 300ml full-fat milk in a pan with a split vanilla pod to just below boiling point, then remove from the heat and leave to infuse for 10 minutes. Crack 5 large egg yolks into a bowl and mix in 30g caster sugar and 2 teaspoons cornflour. Reheat the liquid and gradually pour over the egg yolks. Put back into a clean pan, remove the vanilla and stir over a very low heat until it thickens. Or use a thermometer and don't let the mixture get above 75°C. Pour into a cold bowl and leave to cool, or serve hot.

Basic pancake batter

For about 15 pancakes, put 125g plain flour in a bowl and make a hollow in the middle. Crack in 2 eggs and stir with a wooden spoon, adding 300ml full-fat milk a little at a time, allowing the flour to fall gradually into the liquid. Stir until smooth and, if you have time, set aside for 15 minutes, then stir in a pinch of salt. Before using the batter, stir and if it feels thicker than double cream add a splash of water. Have ready a small pot containing melted ghee, butter or olive oil by the hob. Roll up some sheets of kitchen paper to dip into the pot to grease the pan. Heat a 20–22cm base frying pan over a medium heat. Pour a few tablespoons of batter into a glass and pour into the pan, tilting it as you go to get a thin even covering. As small holes appear on the surface, check the bottom is golden and flip the pancake with a spatula to cook for a further 30 seconds.

Tip onto a plate, cover with foil and keep warm in a low oven while the rest are cooked, or serve them up as you cook them. Serve with honey or maple syrup or the classic golden caster sugar and lemon juice.

Easy egg pasta

When making pasta, think playtime! It's not crucial to make perfectly symmetrical sheets or strands. Turn it into a fun project and it will feel less daunting. If you invest in a pasta machine it takes the heavy work away, but it's not difficult to roll it thinly and slice by hand. Simply divide the dough into manageable-sized pieces and get rolling. The pasta recipe on page 82 is very pliable and the beetroot powder can be substituted with many other flavours such as spinach, saffron and mushroom powder or omitted entirely. Cook as soon as it has all been rolled and cut, otherwise lay on a tray in a single layer and freeze. Once it has frozen hard, put into bags and label. When ready to use, cook from frozen. Or you can hang it up to dry, then store in jars; but for convenience I prefer freezing.

- ### Duck egg sponge

This is based on a lovely light recipe from Darina
Allen's book *Forgotten Skills*. Preheat the oven to180°C/
gas mark 4. Grease the base and sides of 2 x 18cm cake
tins, dust with a little flour and tap out the excess. Separate
2 duck eggs and whisk the whites with 60g caster sugar
until stiff. Whisk in the yolks, one at a time, then gently fold
in 50g sifted plain flour. Divide the mixture between the
tins and bake for 20 minutes. Leave to cool completely,
then sandwich with jam and whipped cream.

- ### A swift Crème Brulée

Preheat the oven to 170°C/gas 3. Whisk 4 egg yolks, 2
teaspoons cornflour, 1 teaspoon vanilla bean paste and
50g caster sugar to a paste, then stir in 5 tablespoons
milk. Whisk 400ml double cream until just thickening
and mix in. Divide between 6 shallow 150ml gratin
dishes. Bake for 12 minutes until there is only a slight
wobble in the middle. Turn off the heat and set aside
for 5 minutes. When cool, chill in the fridge. Up to an
hour before eating, dust with sugar and heat under the
grill or use a blowtorch until caramelised and crisp.

- ### Quiche Lorraine

Line a 20cm x 3.5cm deep fluted loose-bottomed tin
with a sheet of bought ready-rolled shortcrust pastry
(rolled out a little thinner on a floured surface) Chill for
10 minutes. Put 150g smoked lardons in a cold frying
pan and fry for 5 minutes, then set aside. Preheat the
oven to 220°C/gas mark 7. Crack 1 medium egg into a
bowl and separate another 3 and add the yolks to the
bowl. Whisk in 300ml double cream, a small pinch of
sea salt crystals and black pepper. Lay the cold lardons
in the chilled pastry and set the tin on a heated baking
tray. Pour in the egg mixture and cook for 20 minutes.
Lower the heat by 20°C and cook for 10 minutes more
until puffy and golden.

A little egg know-how

- ### The hen and her egg

There's something quite magical about a hen's egg. It's
a beautifully formed, neatly packaged little container
which, at the point it is laid, has everything in place to
give nourishment to the embryo chick. Whether or not
an egg is fertilised, nature has constructed the perfect
food, the yolk protected by many layers to sustain the
life of the chick right up to the time it hatches. This is
true, of course, of all bird eggs but it is primarily the
humble, hard-working hen that we have to thank for the
eggs most of us enjoy in our daily diet.

The female chicken at 16–24 weeks is a young egg-
laying hen called a pullet. At a year old she becomes a
hen, in general laying about six eggs a week. If an egg
is not taken from the nesting box, a hen may become

'broody' and incubate it for around 21 days, during which time she won't lay any more eggs.

The colour of the eggshell is influenced by genetics, not what the hens are given to eat. The yolk's colour, on the other hand, in those beautiful varying shades of yellow to intense orange, is entirely down to their diet.

• *How an egg is constructed*

The eggshell and inner membranes are not only physical protection for the contents, but they also obstruct microbes penetrating to the yolk. In addition, the exterior of the shell has a protective waxy cuticle or 'bloom' sealing the pores of the shell. Washing eggs removes this protective layer, which is why I don't recommend it, but even if any pathogens do manage to get through the shell and membranes, they face further obstacles: the powerful antibacterial properties of, first, a fine veil of thin albumen, then a mass of very thick albumen, both surrounded by a double membrane.

The egg inside this protective shell contains two very different ingredients: the yolk, mostly protein with some fat, and the albumen (the egg white) totally fat free, and full of protein. The yolks are perfect for enriching and emulsifying fats and liquids that have a reluctance to combine without separating, to obtain a creamy luscious texture, the most common example being mayonnaise.

The whites are easily increased in volume when air is whisked into them to make meringue. When whisked into a stock they will clarify it as the albumen attracts small particles and impurities to ensure a crystal-clear liquid, as in the case of consommé.

As well as the 'bloom' found on the outside of the shell there are two inner membranes of thin yet tough transparent protein. One sticks to the shell and the other to the albumen, protecting it and holding everything together in case of damage. As the freshly laid egg cools the two membranes separate a little at the rounded end, creating an air pocket.

Inside the egg are two white strands that go by the wonderful name of 'chalaza'. These twist in opposite directions at each end of the yolk, connecting it to the tough inner membrane around the albumen. They are the shock absorbers that make sure the yolk is kept central and secure. The stronger the chalaza, the fresher the egg, so if, when you crack open the egg, they are prominent, don't be put off: it's a good sign and it's all good protein.

• *Egg storage*

The original fast food is ingeniously and naturally packaged for maximum freshness. It's a general misconception that eggs must be stored in the fridge. Of course, depending on where you are in the world, there are different rules and directives for egg production and storage. So, without potentially turning our hero of the kitchen into a hand grenade, we must just touch on the thorny question of how best to store your freshly bought or collected eggs.

The confusion for us as consumers arises because the instructions given on egg boxes that have been bought off the unchilled shelf in the supermarket state that we should refrigerate eggs after purchase! Supermarkets stock eggs on shelves when the average temperature in a store is above the temperature of a fridge. Domestic fridges often have a place for eggs in the door of the fridge. This is the worst place to store them as they will undergo continual movement and temperature change. I'm with the hen here; after all, she has been laying eggs for a lot longer than we've had fridges. Having got to grips with the extent to which Nature goes to ensure the newly laid egg is protected from bacteria and rapid deterioration, I'm personally reassured that eggs don't need to be kept chilled.

I do bring meat and fish that I store in the fridge to room temperature before cooking – otherwise the cooking timings would be inaccurate, and the same is true of eggs, especially the yolks. Very cold eggs just don't cook well. So get ingredients out of the fridge and cook spontaneously. Instinctively, I have never been a fan of chilling eggs, and perhaps that's because I use them so regularly in my cooking that eggs don't sit around for long in my kitchen. Having decided to cook a soft-boiled breakfast egg, or on the spur of the moment to make a quick frittata for lunch, it seems crazy to have to wait an hour for a few eggs to reach room temperature. If you have a lot of eggs, it makes sense to store them away from the heat of the sun or hot spaces.

If you really feel you must chill fresh eggs, get them out of the fridge an hour before you need them and take out only as many as you may need, otherwise they will go off much faster. Of course, even stored correctly out of the fridge, eggs deteriorate over time, so make sure you use any eggs well within the date stamped on the shell and carton. The 'best before' date could be anything up to 28 days from the date of laying.

I have read that a quick way to bring fridge-chilled eggs to room temperature is to put them into warm water. I wouldn't suggest following this advice, as warming eggs is potentially harmful, also it makes the shell less protective if not used straight away.

How to store the perfect egg

The egg, packaged so beautifully and simply in a protective yet vulnerable shell, needs considerate treatment.

Overchilling causes the shell's waterproof cuticle or 'bloom' to dissolve as the egg pores sweat and become damp. Washing has the same effect, because as soon as this 'bloom' is washed off the shell becomes porous and vulnerable and the egg's freshness can be compromised. This is why washing eggs is not a good idea. Another key function of the 'bloom' is to keep the pH of the egg constant. If the 'bloom' is lost, the alkaline quality of the egg increases as carbon dioxide diffuses from the egg into the air. This negatively affects the structure of the proteins within the egg and causes more rapid deterioration. So it's fine to store the bulk of your eggs in a cool shady place, and it's also nice to have a few in a bowl in the kitchen if very fresh: they look so beautiful and inviting, just as nice as a bowl of fruit or a vase of flowers.

Finally, when I do take my eggs out of the carton I make sure they sit rounded end uppermost. This is the end where the air pocket is located and keeping the eggs round-end up prevents the weight of the egg rupturing the membrane.

The very best eggs

How the eggs you buy are produced is as important as the provenance of any meat or vegetable. Always make sure you have the best eggs to cook with. If you buy organic eggs laid by happily clucking free-range hens (or, better still, Soil Association organic-standard eggs, as the hens are moved to fresh ground more often), you will get the very best from your eggs. Buying eggs from caged birds often fed an unnatural diet is totally unacceptable for the hen, and for the consumer. To be healthy a hen needs a balanced diet of greenery, worms, grains and grubs and to be able to scratch around in the earth. Pastured eggs, just like dairy produce from grass-fed cows, are much more nutritious than eggs from poorly raised hens confined to cages or barns.

In the UK, the Red Lion food safety mark stamped on eggs guarantees they are laid by hens that were vaccinated as chicks against salmonella. Washing or keeping eggs chilled does not stop salmonella, because if a hen has the bacteria her eggs will already have been infected before the shell is formed. Good hen-keeping practice helps to keep salmonella away. The priority should be to produce clean eggs at the point of collection, rather than trying to clean them afterwards. This is standard practice for those who care about the welfare of their laying birds. If you are lucky enough to be given eggs by friends who keep hens, or you buy at the farm gate, or at farmers' markets, don't worry if the shells are a little dirty and don't wash them. Just buff off any bits with a dry rough cloth just before carefully cracking the eggs into a bowl and use them to cook with right away. Then bin the cloth used to wipe them with and wash your hands well in hot soapy water before you do anything else. It's best to wash your hands automatically after cracking any egg.

EU and UK egg marketing laws state that Class 'A' eggs, for example those found on supermarket shelves, must not be washed or cleaned in any way. The understanding behind this is that it encourages good practice on the part of egg-producing farms because no one wants to buy dirty eggs. Laws in the USA and some other countries require eggs to be washed in a mild sanitising solution, then dried thoroughly and coated with a flavourless mineral oil to mimic the natural cuticle or 'bloom'. They are then kept in the chiller cabinet in stores. Eggs sold in farmers' markets are not routinely subject to such regulations.

A full avian line-up

• *Everyday eggs*

Hen eggs – in season year round. The shells come in white, all shades of brown and buff, sometimes speckled, pale blue and green. The colour of the shell depends entirely on the breed of hen.

Pullet eggs – in season all year round. Pullets are young hens aged between 16 and 24 weeks, so the eggs are small with a comparatively large yolk. At around 1 year a pullet matures to become a hen.

Bantam eggs – in season year round. This is a small rare breed of hen that produces a very cute, small-size egg – great for children. The colour is usually off-white.

Duck eggs – in season year round. The shells are very white, pale grey or greeny blue with an attractive translucence despite being very tough to crack open. Use 1 duck egg for each hen egg, or if a recipe requires a lot of eggs use 2 duck to 3 hen eggs. The white of a duck egg is often slightly cloudy and pearlised – they poach beautifully and are very good for sponges.

Quail eggs – in season year round. They have dainty and glamorously speckled, pale buff-coloured shells each with a unique pattern. The flavour is much like that of a hen egg but the yolk is often paler. For a bit of fun, quail eggs are delicious boiled and served with mock caviar or, for a special night, the real deal!

- *Glamorous eggs*

Guinea fowl eggs – in season late spring–late summer. Guinea fowl lay only around 1 egg each week. Their eggs are smaller and rounder than hens' in varying shades of oatmeal, often slightly speckly. The shells are so hard they feel almost fake.

Pheasant eggs – in season late spring–mid-summer. The shells can be khaki, olive green or green blue, like an exclusive paint shade card. They are half the size and have a stronger flavour than a hen egg but are wonderful poached with flavoured crunchy salt flakes.

Goose eggs – in season early spring–mid-summer. The shell is whitish and very hard yet elegantly shaped and around three times the size of a hen egg. The large yolks are perfect for mayonnaise and ideal to soft-boil for two to share.

Turkey eggs – in season late spring–mid-summer. About the size of a duck egg and the palest of buff colour with fine speckles. Turkeys don't lay many eggs.

- *Outrageous eggs*

Partridge eggs – in season late spring–mid-summer. Pretty little squat eggs in delicious shades of beige with coffee-coloured speckles.

Gull eggs – protection laws are enforced and only a certain number of black-headed gull eggs can be collected from the wild by those with a licence during a one-month window, usually late April–May in the UK. Gull eggs have a beautiful green speckly shell and are a delicacy: rich in flavour, not fishy, with whites a dense pearly white. They soft-boil very well, and are lovely dished up with a ghee hollandaise.

- *Epic eggs*

Rhea eggs – the rhea is a flightless South American bird similar to an ostrich. One egg is about the equivalent of 10 hen eggs. Stronger in flavour but light in texture, they are great for heavier tortillas and frittatas.

Ostrich eggs – a single egg is the equivalent of 24 hen eggs, so will feed around 8 people for a scramble. They have hard-to-crack, very tough shells. If you are thinking about soft-boiling, they take around 50 minutes and have quite a pronounced flavour.

Emu – from the second-largest bird in the world, the eggs have beautiful dark green and very tough shell about 14cm long. Emus lay about 55 eggs each season. With a massive yolk and fluffy texture, they make a great scramble for a gathering.

Breakfasts & Snacks

baked

Cheese & nigella seed muffins with herb & nut butter

This makes enough herb and nut butter for another dish. Great to spread on toast and topped with a poached egg for a really speedy snack.

makes 12 (with enough butter left for another dish)

250g white spelt flour
1 teaspoon baking powder
½ teaspoon bicarbonate of soda
½ teaspoon English mustard powder
¾ teaspoon nigella seeds
175g Double Gloucester cheese, freshly grated
50g Parmesan cheese, freshly grated
300ml buttermilk
4 medium eggs
sea salt crystals and freshly ground white pepper

For the herb and nut butter
125g salted butter, softened
10g flat-leaf parsley, leafy sprigs removed and chopped
8 walnut halves, finely chopped

To make the herb and nut butter, mix all the ingredients together and spoon into small dishes. Smooth the tops and chill.

Preheat the oven to 200°C/gas mark 6. Line a 12-hole muffin tin with paper muffin cases, placing two cases in each hole.

Sift the dry ingredients into a bowl, then mix in the nigella seeds, cheeses and seasoning.

Put the buttermilk in a bowl, crack in the eggs and whisk together. Make a well in the middle of the flour mixture and pour in the liquid, mixing until just combined. Divide between the muffin cases and bake in the oven for 20 minutes until risen and golden. Serve hot or cold with the chilled herb and nut butter.

from the pan

Dan's super complète – a crêpe with ham, egg & cheese

The lack of gluten in buckwheat makes this a useful recipe for those sensitive to wheat as, despite its name, buckwheat is a fruit seed from the rhubarb family, not a grain. Buckwheat flour is rich in minerals and vitamins and gives these crêpes (or galettes) a pleasant nutty flavour. There is no need to rest the batter but you can keep what you don't use in the fridge and make more crêpes the next day to have with perhaps scrambled eggs and smoked salmon or honey and lemon. I like to use good-quality ghee to get a golden crêpe every time, but butter is fine to use. This is my son Dan's favourite breakfast, always ordered in the best French accent!

enough to make 10–16 crêpes about 20–22cm

125g buckwheat flour
¼ teaspoon sea salt crystals
3 medium eggs
400ml full-fat milk
75g ghee

To serve (per crêpe)
45g ready-sliced
 good-quality ham
35g Gruyère cheese, grated, or
 2 slices of Emmental
1 small egg

Line an oven tray with foil followed by baking paper; have on hand another sheet of each for covering the hot crêpes.

Sift the flour into a medium bowl and make a well in the middle.

Whisk the salt, eggs and milk together. Add about a quarter of the mixture to the flour and whisk in the middle, allowing the flour to fall naturally into the liquid (this avoids lumps). As the mixture thickens add more liquid until all the flour falls in and is whisked to a super-smooth batter. Melt 30g of the ghee in a small pan and whisk into the batter.

Heat a 20–22cm frying pan over a high heat, then lower to medium. Add some hard ghee using the tip of a knife – you want two small knobs to begin with. When it melts, ladle in some batter (or measure 4–5 tablespoons into a glass and pour from that) – you can judge from this first crêpe how much is best.

Instantly swirl the pan so the batter coats the base right to the edges and cook for about a minute (it helps to fluctuate the heat between medium and low). Lift the crêpe onto a spatula (it is sturdy enough to do this) and add another small knob of ghee moving it across the pan with the knife. Cook the other side for about a minute.

Transfer to the lined tray as you continue to cook the number of crêpes you want and cover with the baking paper and foil. They remain very

pliable and won't stick together, so just pile one on top of the other. They can be reheated all at once if need be (see below).

Put one of the crêpes into the frying pan and put some ham in the middle. Make a nest with the cheese on top and crack in a small egg. Bring the sides of the crêpe over the fillings so just the egg is exposed and place the pan over a low–medium heat. Cover with a lid and cook for about 3 minutes so the egg cooks to your liking and the cheese melts. Repeat for the other crêpes.

Alternatively, preheat the oven to 200°C/ gas mark 6 and prepare all the filled crêpes together, putting them straight onto a baking sheet. Cover with a foil tent so it doesn't touch the filling but does leave space to create steam. Bake in the oven for about 5 minutes or until the eggs cook to your liking.

baked

Corn & chorizo taco cups

It's nice to use corn tortillas for this recipe but you could use the wheat-flour type instead. Spinach is an alternative to curly kale – just make certain you squeeze every drop of moisture from any cooked leaves before adding to the eggs. Any suitable hard cheese is fine as a substitute for the manchego.

makes 6 taco cups

100g soft cooking chorizo
   sausage
1 tablespoon rapeseed oil, plus
   extra for greasing
1 garlic clove, crushed to a paste
   with a few sea salt crystals
100g curly kale, leaves stripped
   off the thick stems and sliced
1 corn cob
2 teaspoons wholegrain mustard
75ml full-fat milk
5 medium eggs
100g Manchego cheese, finely
   grated
6 small soft corn tortillas
handful of small coriander sprigs
sea salt crystals and freshly
   ground black pepper

Pull the skin off the chorizo and cut the sausage into small cubes. Heat a frying pan and dry-fry the sausage for a few minutes until the oil flows out. Tip onto a tray lined with kitchen paper and wipe the pan clean. Heat the oil over a medium heat and add the garlic, then, as soon as it sizzles, add the curly kale and stir-fry for a few minutes. Put on a lid and cook for a further few minutes. Tip into a colander and leave to drain.

Stand the corn cob upright on a board and slice off the corn kernels, cutting down in one go with a sharp knife. Put in a pan of boiling salted water and cook for 5 minutes. Drain and refresh in cold water and drain again. Tip onto the tray with the chorizo.

Preheat the oven to 180°C/gas mark 4. Put the mustard in a large bowl and gradually mix in the milk. Crack in the eggs and whisk with a fork to break them up, mix in the cheese and season. Lightly grease a 6-hole muffin tin with the extra oil. If you wish, use scissors to trim about 1cm all round from each tortilla and gently fold and push into the greased tin.

Squeeze all the moisture from the curly kale and add to the egg mixture along with the chorizo and corn. Fold in gently. Ladle an even amount into each tortilla case and bake in the oven for 10 minutes. Lower the heat to 160°C/gas mark 3 and bake for a further 5–10 minutes until puffed and firm when pressed. Serve scattered with coriander sprigs.

fried

Hot ham- & cheese eggy bread

These are my version of *emparedados calientes* – hot sandwiches – found on the snack menu of all good Spanish tapas bars. They really hit the spot along with a few olives, some cheeky padrón peppers and ice-cold beer.

enough for 2–4

8 slices of bread
8 slices of Serrano or other
    dry-cured ham
12 thin chorizo slices (cooked)
60g Manchego or other hard
    cheese, finely grated
4 large eggs
2 tablespoons milk
6 tablespoons extra virgin olive oil
sea salt crystals and freshly
    ground black pepper

Cut the crusts off the bread if you want (it looks neater) and lay out four of the slices. Divide the ham and chorizo between the slices and scatter with pepper. Add the cheese, top with the rest of the bread and sandwich together.

Crack the eggs into a flat dish and whisk in the milk and a pinch of salt. Add two of the sandwiches and turn them in the egg mixture. Heat half the oil in a frying pan large enough to take two at a time and fry on both sides until golden and crispy. Repeat the soaking and frying of the rest.

Cut into triangles and pierce with a cocktail stick to keep them together. Serve right away while hot.

fried

Fried halloumi & egg

I found this some time ago in Claudia Roden's book *Middle Eastern Food* and loved the combination so much I frequently make it for a swift snack. It must be eaten right away while the halloumi is still soft and the egg just cooked. I like it with a bunch of rocket on the side.

enough for 1

1 teaspoon olive oil
knob of butter
2–3 slices of halloumi, 5mm thick
1 duck egg
pul biber red pepper flakes or
    freshly ground black pepper
sea salt crystals (optional)

Heat a small frying pan (base about 15cm) and add the oil and butter. Fry the halloumi on one side for a few minutes until golden, then turn and fry for a further minute. Crack in the egg and cook it to your liking. Add the red pepper flakes and serve with salt if wished, bearing in mind the halloumi is quite salty.

soft boiled

Asian-Scotch eggs

Here's my take on the sausagemeat-encased egg snack, made with seafood and Asian spices fried to a crispy coating. You can buy boxes of eggs in mixed sizes, which is useful for this recipe as you can use the smallest and largest. Panko crumbs, common in Japanese cooking, instantly give an almost glamorous golden finish. A tip to clean out your blender after making the paste is to soak, then rinse, in cold water before washing it in hot soapy water, otherwise the protein sticks like glue.

enough for 6

250g raw peeled prawns,
    deveined and roughly chopped
200g skinless cod or haddock
    fillet, roughly chopped
1 lemongrass stem, trimmed and
    finely chopped
pinch of turmeric powder
pinch of sea salt crystals
1 large egg yolk
1 red chilli, deseeded and
    finely chopped
10g coriander, leaves removed
    and finely chopped
6 small eggs

For frying
1 large egg
1 large egg white
2 teaspoons milk
55g plain flour
85g fresh breadcrumbs or
    panko crumbs
250ml olive oil or 250g raw
    coconut oil, melted

To serve
sweet chilli sauce
tomato ketchup
dressed green salad leaves

Put the prawns, cod, lemongrass, turmeric, a pinch of sea salt crystals and egg yolk in a mini blender (you may need to do this in two batches) and whizz to a paste. Tip into a bowl, mix in the chilli and coriander, then chill.

Have two bowls of cold water ready. Pour boiling water into a pan just large enough to take the six eggs in a single layer. Place over a medium heat and bring back to the boil. Lower the heat so the water isn't moving and add the eggs (this stops cracking), then turn up the heat to simmer for 5 minutes, giving a soft yolk – if you want it firmer, simmer for 7 minutes.

Lift the eggs out with a slotted spoon into one of the bowls of cold water. Immediately gently crack the rounded end and peel carefully while still hot – the shell comes off easily done this way. Put each peeled egg into the other bowl of cold water.

Crack the whole egg into another bowl, add the egg white and milk and whisk with a fork. Put the flour in one flat dish and the breadcrumbs in another. Line them up: first flour, egg, then breadcrumbs nearest the hob.

Line a plate with kitchen paper and preheat the oven to 160°C/gas mark 3.

Take the prawn mixture out of the fridge and divide it into six portions. Drain the peeled eggs and sit them on kitchen paper. Prepare one egg at a time for frying. Dredge the egg with flour, then, with damp hands, take a portion of the prawn mixture, flatten it on the palm of your hand and put the egg on top. Mould the mixture evenly around the egg, gently easing it to cover completely. Right away dust in flour, then swiftly transfer to the bowl of whisked egg, cover evenly and place it straight into the crumbs. Here you can mould it a little more, now that it's more stable.

Heat the oil in a small, deep pan over a medium heat and, when a crumb of bread sizzles golden, add the coated egg and time 2 minutes. Baste and turn the egg gently to cook evenly all round. Give it another minute, if needs be, to get nice and golden. Transfer to the lined oven tray and continue to coat and cook the other eggs in the same way. To eat hot, put them in the oven for 3 minutes.

Serve hot or cold with some sweet chilli sauce and tomato ketchup stirred together to make a dipping sauce, and some dressed green salad leaves.

fried

Frazzled wok eggs on toast with grilled tomatoes, black pudding & dukkah

The Egyptian spice mix dukkah keeps well in a sealed jar and is very handy to scatter over lots of dishes. Find it in the spice aisle in supermarkets and customise it by adding your own exciting extras. I like to use Irish black pudding made with oatmeal for this dish.

enough for 2

50g–70g packet of dukkah
1 teaspoon pul biber red
    pepper flakes
2 tablespoons pistachio nibs
    or skinned pistachios,
    roughly crushed
7 tablespoons extra virgin olive oil
150–200g good-quality black
    pudding, skinned
2 slices of bread
2–3 tomatoes, cored
    and quartered
2 large eggs
freshly ground black pepper

Tip the dukkah into a bowl and mix in the red pepper flakes and crushed pistachios. Heat 2 teaspoons of the olive oil in a frying pan over a medium heat, crumble in the black pudding and stir-fry for 2 minutes.

Meanwhile, preheat the grill to high and line a baking sheet with foil. Place the bread and the tomatoes, cut-side up, on the baking sheet, grind over some pepper and spoon over a tablespoon of the olive oil. Grill for about 1½ minutes, turn the toast and continue to grill for about a minute until golden. Remove the toast and leave the tomatoes to finish for maybe a minute. Spoon a little more olive oil over the toast and keep everything warm in the switched-off grill.

Heat a large wok and, when it smokes, add all but a tablespoon of the remaining olive oil. Crack an egg into a cup and add to the oil (watch it carefully as it will spit a lot). Spoon over the oil and coax the white to fold over the yolk. When the white has frazzled golden edges and the yolk is set to your liking, lift it onto a plate lined with kitchen paper. Fry the second egg in the same way.

Serve the black pudding with the tomatoes on the slices of toast, and top each with an egg golden-side up. Spoon over the last of the olive oil and scatter with the dukkah.

baked

Toast, egg & bacon muffin tin bakes

A mini breakfast in a muffin tin and you can even prepare it the night before – come morning, just add eggs, scatter over the chives and bake.

enough for 6

3 large slices of good bread
½ teaspoon olive oil
12 thin smoked streaky bacon
 rashers – or pancetta
45g vintage Cheddar cheese, finely
 grated, or a hard goat's cheese
6 medium eggs
8 chives, finely snipped
pul biber red pepper flakes or
 freshly ground black pepper
sea salt crystals

Preheat the oven to 200°C/ gas mark 6. Toast the bread on both sides and cut out two rounds from each slice to fit the bases of a 6-hole muffin tin. Use the oil to brush around the tin, pop in the toast rounds and season with salt and a few pepper flakes or ground pepper. Grill the bacon for about a minute on each side so it's not quite cooked but still pliable.

Arrange two of the bacon rashers around the edges of each hole of the muffin tin to make cosy nests for the eggs. Divide the cheese between them, press down and crack an egg into each. Add the chives and pepper flakes and bake in the oven for around 10 minutes until the eggs are set to your liking. Scatter with salt as you eat.

souffléd

Cheesy kale & nut fritters
with tomato vinaigrette

This is such a great way to use up egg whites. The whites create a fluffy souffléd binding for the other nutritious ingredients. Dip the fritters into the tomato vinaigrette to munch on. Any you don't eat will reheat beautifully the next day, loosely wrapped in foil in a preheated hot oven for 4 minutes.

makes 16

150–200g curly kale on stalks (around 125g off the stalks)
2 garlic cloves, crushed to a paste with a few sea salt crystals
100g Gruyère cheese
50g breadcrumbs (or whizz up a slice of crustless bread) – not too fine
3 tablespoons pine nuts, roughly chopped
freshly ground black pepper
6 medium egg whites
250ml olive oil

For the tomato vinaigrette
4 tablespoons extra virgin olive oil
2 garlic cloves, crushed to a paste with a few sea salt crystals
1 red chilli, deseeded and chopped
250g ripe tomatoes, deseeded and chopped
1 tablespoon white balsamic vinegar or wine vinegar
freshly ground black pepper

To make the tomato vinaigrette, put half the oil in a pan over a medium heat and add the garlic and as soon as the garlic sizzles (not browns), stir to break up and add the chilli, tomatoes and black pepper and cook over a lowish heat for 5 minutes. Cool slightly, then add the vinegar and the rest of the oil, transfer to a blender and whizz to a purée. Pass through a sieve set over a bowl.

Pull the kale leaves off the thick stems in pieces and blanch in boiling salted water for 2 minutes. Drain and refresh under cold water. Squeeze out the excess water and lay on a clean tea towel to dry for 5 minutes. Put in a bowl, add the garlic and finely grate the Gruyère into the kale, mixing it in as you go. Add the breadcrumbs, pine nuts and black pepper to taste.

Preheat the oven to 120°C/gas mark ¼. Whisk the egg whites until the beaters leave a pattern in the foam. Gently and evenly fold into the kale mixture. Don't worry if it loses a little volume. Divide roughly into about 16 heaps – not too large and not too perfect – use a tablespoon if you want.

Add the oil to a medium, deep-sided pan over a medium heat and when it's hot (you may have to keep adjusting the heat so the fritters don't brown too quickly), fry about three fritters at a time for about 2–2½ minutes per side until beautifully golden. Transfer the fritters as they are cooked to a baking tray lined with kitchen paper and keep them warm in the oven until all are cooked. Serve with the tomato vinaigrette.

scrambled

Scandi spring scramble

Use lovely, fresh spring vegetables to make this. Young broad beans don't need skinning when they're tender. I like my scramble softish, but just firming up – remember the eggs continue to cook in their own heat, so don't leave them hanging about in the pan. Serve on a thin buckwheat crêpe (see page 24) or with thin slices of toasted rye bread, if you like.

enough for 3–4

100g shelled broad beans
50g shelled fresh peas
6 medium eggs
4 tablespoons full-fat milk
120g thinly sliced smoked salmon
15g butter
75g soft goat's cheese
50g pea shoots
1 lime, cut into wedges (optional)
sea salt crystals and freshly
   ground black pepper

Cook the broad beans and peas in boiling salted water for 2–3 minutes. Drain and refresh in cold water to stop them cooking.

Crack the eggs into a bowl and whisk in the milk and seasoning. Tear the salmon into pieces and set aside.

Melt the butter in a large-based pan or frying pan over a medium heat. When it starts to sizzle pour in the egg mixture and stir with a wooden spoon, scraping the cooked egg into the runny mixture from around the edges as it sets. Continue to stir into curds for about 2 minutes until the mixture is as you like a scramble to be.

Scatter over the beans and peas and fold in with the salmon. Serve, topped with scoops of soft goat's cheese and pea shoots, with a wedge of lime to squeeze over and an extra sprinkling of ground pepper, if you wish.

poached

Cilbir

This recipe was found in a dusty old Turkish cookbook I relegated to the top shelf of my foodie library some time back. I have been making it in some form or another for years and this is the recent update. It's something really quite wonderful for its speed, simplicity and exoticness.

enough for 2

175g thick natural full-fat yogurt
1 garlic clove, crushed to a paste
   with a few sea salt crystals
1 tablespoon hummus
15g ghee
8 sage leaves
large pinch of sweet paprika
2 duck eggs
splash of wine vinegar
pul biber red pepper flakes or
   chilli flakes
4 pieces of the thinnest toast you
   can make from your best bread,
   to serve

Mix the yogurt, garlic and hummus together and divide between two bowls.

Heat the ghee in a small pan and fry the sage leaves for a few seconds, then lift onto kitchen paper. Add the sweet paprika to the ghee and set aside.

Break a duck egg into a cup. Get some water boiling in a medium pan, add the vinegar and swirl the water. Lower the first egg into the middle of the swirl, turn off the heat and time 3 minutes. When it is ready lift out with a slotted spoon and place it, still on the spoon, on kitchen paper to drain. Crack the next egg into the cup and cook in the same way.

While it cooks, heat the ghee again briefly and spoon onto the bowls of yogurt mixture. Lay the drained poached egg on top of one bowl, scatter with sage leaves and some red pepper flakes and serve with the toast. Finish the second egg in the same way, then eat before it gets cold.

More options for toppings
Skin 1 small or 3 cocktail chorizo, break them up and fry in a dry pan, drain on kitchen paper and scatter over the yogurt mixture. Fry some parsley leaves in oil for about 30 seconds, drain on kitchen paper and scatter over the dish. Scatter with dukkah instead of red pepper flakes (see recipe page 32). Use the anchovy, olive and caper salsa from page 80.

batter

Egg-battered prawns with crispy spring onion & chilli

Just add some wasabi to soy sauce and serve as a dip if you don't want the crispy additions, but for me they're the best bit. Add lots of coriander leaves as you serve.

enough for 4

24 raw prawns, peeled, with tails left on
1 lime
olive oil, for frying
2 long red chillies, deseeded (if you wish) and finely sliced
5 spring onions, trimmed and finely sliced
2 large eggs
2 teaspoons cornflour, plus extra for dusting
sea salt crystals and freshly ground black pepper
coriander leaves, to serve

Butterfly the prawns by slitting along the belly (taking out the black vein if there is one) but not all the way through. Cut the lime in half, squeeze the juice over the prawns and set aside for around 15 minutes. Season with salt and pepper.

Heat a wok, add a tablespoon of the oil and fry the chillies and spring onions until crispy. Drain on kitchen paper.

Crack the eggs into a bowl, season, add the cornflour and whisk with a fork. Sift the cornflour for dusting onto a plate. Drain the prawns and pat dry, dust them all with the flour, avoiding the tail shell if possible. Wipe out the wok and heat about 1cm more oil. Dip a few prawns at a time into the egg and fry for 2–3 minutes, until puffy and a pale golden colour. Serve scattered with the chillies, spring onions and coriander leaves.

scrambled

Tomato toasts with scrambled eggs, herbs & olives

A quick, tasty recipe for a small gathering at breakfast time. I find the charred bread from the griddle pan important to give a smoky flavour, but feel free simply to toast the bread under the grill. The tomatoes take no time just to heat through – don't overcook them otherwise the skins loosen and that's not what you want. I prefer my scrambled eggs to have a bit of texture, but if you prefer a uniform creamy texture you could make them in a bain-marie (see page 10).

enough for 6

3 short French sticks, each halved
   lengthways
2 whole garlic cloves, peeled
6 tablespoons extra virgin olive oil,
   plus extra to serve
750g ripe tomatoes
3 garlic cloves, crushed to a paste
   with a few sea salt crystals
1 teaspoon pul biber red pepper
   flakes or freshly ground
   black pepper
8 medium eggs
8 oregano or marjoram sprigs,
   some in flower if possible, leaves
   and flowers removed
18 Kalamata olives, sliced off the
   stones in slivers
freshly ground black pepper
small pinch of sea salt crystals

Heat a ridged griddle pan over a high heat and toast the bread on the cut sides. Generously rub the toasted sides with the whole garlic cloves right to the edges of the bread and spoon over the extra virgin olive oil.

Halve, core and roughly chop the tomatoes, then drain through a colander set over a bowl (keep the juice to drink). Once they are well drained, put 3 tablespoons of the olive oil and the garlic in a frying pan and set over a high heat. As soon the garlic sizzles, stir and quickly add the tomatoes so the garlic doesn't brown; cook for 3 minutes without stirring just to heat through rather than break them down. Mix in the red pepper flakes or black pepper.

Meanwhile, crack the eggs into a bowl, break up with a fork and mix in a small pinch of salt. When the tomatoes are ready, make the scramble. Heat a large pan (preferably non-stick) over a low–medium heat and add the rest of the oil. Pour in the eggs and stir constantly over a low heat using a wooden spoon to scrape the cooked egg into the runny mixture from the bottom of the pan and around the edges as it sets. Continue to stir into wet curds for about 2 minutes or until the mixture is as you like a scramble to be.

Chop half the oregano or marjoram and fold into the tomato mixture. Very lightly fold the scramble through the tomato mixture and spoon it onto the toasts. Scatter with the olive slivers and the rest of the oregano or marjoram leaves (and flowers if you have them). Spoon over more extra virgin olive oil to serve.

batter

Easy-peasy hot cakes

Peas from the freezer are great for this last-minute quick recipe along with half a drained can of whatever white bean you have in the cupboard. Eat hot or warm with smoked fish and salad. They look cute – like green blinis, but without gluten and yeast.

enough for 4–6 (makes about 18)

125g frozen peas, defrosted in hot water and rinsed in cold
100g canned haricot beans, drained and rinsed
2 mint sprigs
1 tablespoon buckwheat flour
3 medium eggs
75g hard goat's cheese or Parmesan, finely grated
½ teaspoon caraway seeds, freshly ground
1 tablespoon olive oil
½ teaspoon sea salt crystals

To serve
pinch of caraway seeds, roughly crushed
150g crème fraîche
10cm piece of cucumber, deseeded and thinly sliced into short ribbons
½ teaspoon sea salt crystals
1 teaspoon honey
5 radishes, thinly sliced
1 small red onion, halved and thinly sliced
1 tablespoon white balsamic vinegar
smoked fish, such as trout, salmon, halibut or mackerel
dill fronds

For the sides, mix the caraway into the crème fraîche in a small bowl and chill. Put the cucumber ribbons in a bowl, mix in the salt and leave for 10 minutes. Drain, pat dry and add the honey, radishes, onion and vinegar, toss to mix and chill until needed.

For the hot cakes, tip the peas into a blender with the haricot beans, mint and buckwheat flour. Crack the eggs into a bowl and add to the blender with the cheese, caraway and salt (if using Parmesan instead of hard goat's cheese, you will need less salt) and pulse to a purée.

Heat a frying pan over a medium heat, add a little oil and wipe out with kitchen paper (you don't want the cakes to swim in oil – just a smear is enough). Add a spoonful or small ladleful of the pea mixture to the pan, enough to form a cake about 6cm in diameter. Cook four at a time. Turn the heat right down and cook for 1½ minutes, then gently flip them over with a palette knife and cook for a further minute until lightly golden in parts and firm to the touch.

If you want them warm, wrap in foil and put in a warm oven while you cook the rest. Serve the hot cakes with the fish, crème fraîche and cucumber salad, scattered with dill fronds.

boiled

Pickled quail eggs Thai-style

Use a gentle white balsamic vinegar for the pickle rather than a harsh-tasting cheap one. These are ready to eat after just 24 hours but you can eat them from the fridge for up to three days. Serve them with cashews, stir-fried in a hot wok until evenly golden then scattered with sea salt crystals and chopped red chilli. Eat with a long glass of Chang beer and be transported to a beach in Thailand.

enough for 4–6

12–24 quail eggs
150ml white balsamic vinegar
3 tablespoons caster sugar
1 lemongrass stem, thinly sliced diagonally
100ml water
4 kaffir lime leaves, finely shredded
1 long thin red chilli, sliced into rings
2 purple Thai or pink shallots, sliced into rounds

Fill a pan with boiling water and lower the heat before gently putting four or six eggs at a time into the water (this avoids cracking the shell). Turn up the heat to a simmer for 3 minutes. Lift the eggs into a bowl of cold water and continue cooking the rest. Straight away, crack and peel the cooked eggs from the rounded end (it's easier this way).

Put half the white balsamic vinegar in a small pan with the sugar and lemon grass. Dissolve the sugar over a low heat. Turn off the heat and add the rest of the vinegar and the water, the kaffir shreds, chilli and shallots.

Put half the eggs in a clean jar, add some of the vinegar mixture and the other ingredients, then continue to layer up and finish with a covering of vinegar. Cover with a lid and leave to cool completely. Chill and keep for up to three days.

from the pan

Eggs in space with tomato salsa & bacon

This touch of fun has been in my repertoire since the days of small boys, often involving a moustache and some eyebrows. Such a tasty iconic eggie breakfast (the title came from the Allen boys), great with this tomato salsa – you will taste the difference – use tomato ketchup if you must!

enough for 4

2 red tomatoes
2 yellow tomatoes
40g ghee or rapeseed oil
2 long slices of bread (I use
    Puglian durum wheat toasting
    bread) or 4 smaller slices
4 medium eggs
8 streaky bacon rashers
freshly ground black pepper

Quarter the tomatoes, deseed, slice the flesh off the skins and finely chop. Heat a couple of knobs of ghee in a small pan and add the tomatoes, season with pepper and cook for a few minutes until thickened.

Cut two holes of 6cm diameter in each slice of bread with a cookie cutter or a thin glass, keeping the circles in place for frying. Heat the rest of the ghee in a large frying pan over a low–medium heat and add the bread slices. Cook until golden, then turn them over. Remove the cut-out circles and add an egg to each hole – fry the cut-outs too on their other side. Cover the pan for a minute, uncover and cook for a further minute until the eggs are cooked to your liking.

Meanwhile grill the bacon and keep it warm. Cut the large bread slices in half and serve with the bacon at the side and the tomato salsa in a small bowl. Use the cut-outs to dip into the yellow yolks or to carry the salsa.

poached

Golden hash browns with poached eggs & smoked salmon

I like my hash browns to be all tumbly and free-form yet crispy in parts – quite similar to bubble and squeak – instead of cubed and fried. I also like crushed caraway seeds added to the mixture. Use smoked trout or mackerel if you like or look for packs of smoked salmon offcuts that are cheaper to buy.

enough for 4

750g maincrop potatoes (Desirée or King Edward), peeled
1 large onion, finely chopped
1 tablespoon plain flour
1 teaspoon caraway seeds, roughly crushed
5 large eggs
2 tablespoons rapeseed oil
sea salt crystals and freshly ground black pepper
smoked salmon, to serve
chopped chives, to serve

Grate the potatoes on the large holes of a box grater, put straight into cold water and swish it around a bit.

Put the onion in a large bowl with the flour and crushed caraway. Drain the potatoes well, put a third at a time into a clean cloth and squeeze every drop of liquid from them. Add to the bowl, crack in one of the eggs, season well and mix.

Heat the oil in a large frying pan over a medium heat. Add the mixture to the pan and flatten it down. Adjust the heat occasionally so the edges don't burn. After about 5 minutes turn the mixture to brown on the other side. When the underside has browned, break up the mixture to brown the middle. Keep hot.

Half-fill a small pan with water and bring to the boil. Have a bowl of cold water on hand. Crack an egg into a small glass and stir the boiling water to create a whirlpool effect. Gently lower the egg into the vortex and turn the heat right down. Cook for 3 minutes. Lift out with a slotted spoon and put in the bowl of cold water. Poach the rest of the eggs in the same way.

When ready to serve, trim any straggly white from the eggs to neaten them up and immerse in a bowl of just-boiled water to warm them up for a minute. When you lift them out with a slotted spoon, rest them on kitchen paper for a second, then transfer them onto the hash brown mixture and serve with smoked salmon and chopped chives.

Marbled tea eggs

These are known as *lu dan* in China and I first ate them in Taiwan as a snack. Try them with a mixture of Chinese five-spice powder and sea salt flakes or some homemade mayonnaise laced with wasabi (see page 14).

makes 6

6 medium eggs
2 tablespoons black tea leaves
6 star anise
200ml dark soy sauce

To serve
½ teaspoon five-spice powder
1 tablespoon sea salt flakes

Put the eggs, tea leaves, star anise and soy in a pan with enough water just to cover the eggs and bring gently to the boil. Turn down to a simmer for 8 minutes, then lift out the eggs and run them under the cold tap to make them easier to handle.

Gently crack them all over to get a crazy-paving effect, but don't remove the shells. Put them back in the hot liquid and simmer for a few more minutes. Turn off the heat and leave the eggs in the liquid to go completely cold before shelling them.

Combine the five-spice powder and sea salt flakes in a small bowl and serve with the beautiful marbled eggs.

boiled

Flower-power paste eggs

Making these Easter or anytime decorated hard-boiled eggs is a tradition in northern England where they are known as paste eggs (or pace eggs as they are called in other areas). They are used in jarping competitions, in which each child holds an egg pointy end up and tries to crack their opponent's egg with one jarp, without breaking their own. Then everyone eats the eggs.

as many eggs as you like,
    preferably white
kitchen paper
papery skins from brown and
    red onions, collected over a
    few weeks
2 sheets of newspaper, or brown
    paper, per egg
edible flowers such as violas,
    primroses or violets (wild ones
    have more pigment in the petals
    so you get a richer colour)
flat-leaf parsley and other herb
    leaves
raffia or string for tying the bundles
light oil such as sunflower oil, to
    seal the finished egg

Sit a few sheets of kitchen paper and some onion skins onto two sheets of newspaper and gently press some flowers and leaves onto your egg shells. Bring the onion skins up and around each egg to cover completely. Dampen the paper and, as tightly as possible without breaking the shell, wrap the newspaper around the egg and tie up with raffia or string.

Place all the wrapped eggs in a large pan and cover with cold water. Bring to a simmer, cook for 12 minutes, then turn off the heat. Lift them out into a large bowl and leave for 15 minutes.

Unwrap the eggs and put into cold water for 5 minutes. Dry them gently and carefully rub with a very small amount of oil. Keep chilled for up to a few days until ready to use.

Brunches
&
Lunches

in the pan

Shakshouka 'my way'

I first cooked this from an Elizabeth David book, *Mediterranean Food,* where it is described as 'chatchouka – a Tunisian dish'. It has since become a very popular egg dish because it's so effortless with its endless variations, so here is my take. Leave out the greens if you want and use spinach instead or mash up a ripe avocado mixed with lime juice to serve on the side with the yogurt.

enough for 4

4 tablespoons rapeseed oil
3 garlic cloves, crushed to a paste
   with a few sea salt crystals
100g spring greens, halved
   lengthways and thinly
   sliced across
500g tomatoes, peeled, deseeded
   and finely chopped
80g roasted piquillo peppers from
   a jar, drained
½ x 400g can chickpeas in water,
   drained and rinsed
4 medium eggs
sea salt crystals and freshly
   ground black pepper
yogurt, to serve

Put 1 tablespoon of the oil in a frying pan with a third of the garlic and heat. When it sizzles add the greens and stir-fry for a minute. Add a splash of water, cover and cook for 2 minutes. Drain and set aside.

Rinse the frying pan; add the rest of the oil and garlic and heat over a medium heat until sizzling. Add the tomatoes and a good grinding of pepper and cook for about 7 minutes until thickened. Finely chop the roasted piquillo peppers and add to the pan along with the chickpeas.

Add the cooked greens in a few piles to heat through. Make nests in the mixture and crack in the eggs, cover and cook for about 4 minutes until the whites are cooked and the yolks are still soft. Serve from the pan with some yogurt to spoon over and a little salt for the eggs.

in the oven

Courgette, ham, egg & feta filo tart

This is just as nice without ham for non-meat eaters and perfect for wrapping up for a jolly picnic, whatever the weather.

enough for 8

75g unsalted butter, plus extra
  for greasing
350g courgettes
225g piece of ham, 8mm thick
200g feta cheese
250g mascarpone cheese
6 large eggs
20g flat-leaf parsley sprigs,
  leaves removed and chopped
220g filo pastry (12 sheets)
sea salt crystals and freshly
  ground black pepper

Preheat the oven to 200°C/gas mark 6. Grease a 20 x 30cm oven tin or dish (sides at least 3.5cm deep) with butter and line with baking paper.

Thinly slice the courgettes and put in a colander, toss with a teaspoon of salt and leave for 20 minutes. Rinse and squeeze to get rid of excess moisture and put on a plate lined with kitchen paper.

Meanwhile, cut the ham into roughly 1cm cubes, crumble the feta into large chunks and put them both in a bowl. Put the mascarpone in a separate bowl and crack in the eggs, one at a time, mixing well to combine. Add the parsley and season.

Melt the butter and lay out four sheets of the filo, brush each with a little of the butter and layer them into the lined tin, allowing them to overhang the edges. Ladle in a little egg and mascarpone mixture and scatter with half the ham, feta and courgettes. Ladle over roughly half the remaining egg mixture and continue layering up until you have used everything. Bring the overhanging pastry up over the mixture.

Brush the remaining eight sheets of filo with a little melted butter. Gently scrunch each sheet onto the top of the mixture in the tin. Bake in the oven for 40 minutes until crisp and golden. Serve hot or cold.

in the oven

Straw potato, cheese & egg stacks

This recipe is a great one for turning out quickly when you're hungry for carbs and also don't fancy any heavy protein. Very simple to make, and if you don't have a mandolin to shred the potato use a grater, with long downward strokes, or even a spiraliser. Fresh, cooked brown shrimps found in packs make a great salty addition to serve with the stacks.

enough for 6 / makes 12

15g salted butter, plus extra for
  greasing
1 tablespoon rapeseed oil
1 medium onion, finely chopped
2 garlic cloves, crushed to a paste
  with a few sea salt crystals
4 tablespoons dry white wine
1kg Desirée potatoes, peeled
3 medium eggs
4 sprigs lemon thyme, leaves
  picked off and chopped
100g medium Cheddar cheese,
  finely grated
sea salt crystals and freshly ground
  black pepper
cooked brown shrimps, to serve
  (optional)

Preheat the oven to 200°C/gas mark 6. Grease a 12-hole muffin tin with butter and line the bases with baking parchment.

Heat the butter and oil in a pan over a low heat and fry the onion for 5 minutes to soften but not brown. Stir in the garlic and wine, then cook to reduce for 4 minutes until thickened. Tip into a large bowl and set aside.

Meanwhile finely shred the potatoes using a mandolin. Crack the eggs into a bowl and break up with a fork. Add the thyme leaves and grated cheese to the onion mixture, along with the eggs and some salt and black pepper. Mix in the potatoes with clean hands to get them well coated with the mixture.

Divide evenly between the muffin-tin holes and bake in the oven for 8 minutes. Lower the heat to 180°C/gas mark 4 and bake for a further 7 minutes or until the potato is soft and the tops golden. Gently remove the potato stacks from the tin and serve hot with the shrimps, if using.

boiled

Gado gado

This easy, Indonesian-based recipe is great for a small gathering – just increase the ingredients, adding others if you want. Have lots of bowls of the peanut sauce as everyone will love it. Make it as spicy as you like by adding extra hot chilli sauce.

enough for 4–6

4–6 medium eggs
500g small salad potatoes
200g thin green beans, stalk end
    removed
200g beansprouts, root trimmed
12cm cucumber, halved lengthways
2 carrots, peeled
small bunch of coriander, leaves
    removed, to serve

For the peanut sauce
150g smooth peanut butter
6 tablespoons cold water
2 garlic cloves, crushed to a paste
    with a few sea salt crystals
2 teaspoons organic coconut
    sugar
1 teaspoon soy sauce
juice of 2 small limes
2 tablespoons fish sauce
2 teaspoons sriracha or other hot
    chilli sauce

First make the peanut sauce. Put the peanut butter in a bowl and beat in the water using a wooden spoon. Add all the remaining ingredients to the bowl.

Bring a pan of water to the boil and lower the heat before gently adding the eggs – this prevents cracking the shell. Immediately increase the heat to a simmer and cook for 7 minutes. Drain the eggs, put into cold water, then crack and peel right away from the rounded end (they are easier to peel while still slightly hot). Pop into cold water while the rest of the salad is prepared.

Cook the potatoes in a pan of boiling salted water for around 15 minutes. Lift out with a slotted spoon and drain in a colander. Add the beans to the water and cook for about 3 minutes until just tender. Lift them out and put them in a bowl. Peel the potatoes, if wished, then cut into rounds the thickness of a coin and add to the beans. Blanch the beansprouts for a few seconds in the water, drain and refresh under cold water.

Slice the cucumber into half-moons. Shave the carrot into ribbons and finely shred lengthways, or shred thinly on a mandolin. Drain and slice the eggs. Spoon each of the ingredients into large, shallow bowls and serve topped with the peanut sauce and coriander leaves.

baked

Coca with eggs flamenco

Coca is a chunky Catalan flatbread with a colourful topping said to resemble the skirts of a flamenco dancer. Try to use Pedro Ximénez sherry in the mix as it's sweet and perfect for this dish. The topping can be made ahead and chilled until you need to cook.

enough for 6

3 tablespoons extra virgin olive oil
1 onion, finely chopped
2 small (about 150g) romano peppers, deseeded and finely chopped
1 small yellow pepper, deseeded and finely chopped
4 garlic cloves, crushed to a paste with a few sea salt crystals
¼ teaspoon freshly ground black pepper
½ teaspoon sweet paprika
6 tomatoes peeled, deseeded and finely chopped
1 tablespoon Pedro Ximénez sherry
3 cocktail-size chorizo sausages (optional), skinned and finely chopped
6 quail eggs or small eggs

For the coca
250g strong white flour, plus extra for dusting
2½ teaspoons fast-action dried yeast
1½ teaspoons sea salt
4 tablespoons extra virgin olive oil
200ml warm water
1 medium egg

First make the flamenco mixture. Heat the olive oil in a medium pan over a medium heat. Add the onion, peppers and garlic, lower the heat and cook for 5 minutes until soft. Add the black pepper, paprika, sherry, and tomatoes and cook over a medium heat for about 15 minutes until it becomes nice and thick, giving the mixture an occasional stir so that it doesn't stick. Add the chopped chorizo, if using. Spoon into a large shallow bowl and set aside to cool completely.

To make the coca, sift the flour into a bowl and mix in the yeast and salt. Make a well in the centre, pour 1 tablespoon olive oil and the warm water and mix with your hands until the dough leaves no trace on the sides of the bowl. Add a little more water if it is too dry. Lightly dust a clean surface with flour and knead the dough until smooth and elastic. Put back in the bowl, cover with clingfilm and leave to rise for about an hour or until doubled in size.

Preheat the oven to 220°C/gas mark 7. Tip the dough onto a lightly floured surface and knead to a flattened ball. Roll out to fit a baking tray about 20 x 30cm, pushing it right to the edges. Brush over a little of the remaining olive oil and make six evenly spaced hollows in the dough. Surround the hollows with the cold flamenco mixture and bake in the oven for 5 minutes.

Press the hollows down again so the dough doesn't rise to fill them up. Bake for 10 minutes more, then crack an egg into each hollow, spoon over the rest of the olive oil and bake for a further 5–10 minutes until the whites become opaque.

Remove from the oven and eat hot or cold – if it gets cold, the egg yolks set, which is also very nice.

poached

A kind of duck eggs benedict

This new take on eggs benedict has all the right components, just not in the right order! But do feel free to go classic with a toasted muffin and spinach. Homemade or good-quality ghee makes a wonderfully well-behaved hollandaise, lasting over hot water for up to 30 minutes.

enough for 4

4 duck eggs
2 tablespoons rapeseed oil
30g butter
1 garlic clove, crushed to a paste
   with a few sea salt crystals
175g crustless bread, whizzed in a
   mini blender to a rough crumb
3 tablespoons freshly chopped
   flat-leaf parsley
2 tablespoons chopped chives
150g curly kale, leaves pulled from
   the tough stalks
150g good-quality sliced ham
freshly ground black pepper

For the ghee hollandaise sauce
150g organic ghee
1 tablespoon white balsamic
   vinegar
2 tablespoons water
3 egg yolks
juice of 1 small lime
sea salt crystals and freshly ground
   black pepper

Half-fill a medium pan with water and bring to the boil. Have a bowl of cold water on hand. Crack an egg into a small glass and stir the boiling water to create a whirlpool effect. Gently lower the egg into the vortex (this compacts the white and helps to cover the yolk in the thick white) and turn the heat right down. Cook for 3 minutes. Lift out with a slotted spoon and put in the bowl of cold water while you continue to cook the rest.

Heat a tablespoon of the oil and the butter in a frying pan, add the garlic and breadcrumbs and fry for about 4 minutes, stirring every few minutes until light golden. Turn off the heat and add the parsley and chives.

In a separate pan, heat the remaining oil and stir-fry the kale for a few minutes. Add a splash of water, cover and cook for another minute until just tender. Remove from the heat and keep warm.

To make the hollandaise, melt the ghee in a small pan until just warm, then transfer to a jug. Put the vinegar, water and a pinch of salt and pepper in the same pan. Add the yolks and whisk until frothy. Put over a very low heat, stirring continuously for 3–4 minutes until just warm (it must not overheat). Remove from the heat. Using electric beaters, whisk in the ghee, starting with dribbles, then in a steady stream whisking continuously until emulsified. Gently stir in the lime juice. Transfer the hollandaise to a basin and sit it over a pan of just-boiled water (heat turned off) without letting the base touch the water. Covered, it will keep warm for up to 30 minutes. You may need to reheat the water after 15 minutes, but remove the bowl to do this, turn off the heat and sit the bowl back over the water and cover.

Trim any straggly white from the eggs to neaten them up and immerse in a bowl of boiling water to warm through for a minute.

Arrange some of the kale on four plates and divide the ham on top. Lift the eggs out using a slotted spoon, drain briefly, then put one on top of each portion and spoon over some hollandaise. Scatter with the crispy crumbs and black pepper.

scrambled

Egg bhurji

A great spicy scrambled-egg-style dish from Pakistan, served with lots of coriander leaves. I like to add freshly squeezed lime juice which is not so acidic as lemon. Take to the table in its cooking pan along with hot flatbreads for scooping. Try adding a little white crabmeat or cooked smoked haddock to warm through for a more substantial meal.

enough for 4

4 large eggs
4 tablespoons full-fat milk
2 tablespoons ghee
2 small onions, finely chopped
2 fat green chillies, deseeded and
   finely sliced
2cm piece of ginger, scraped and
   finely grated
½ teaspoon turmeric powder
¼ teaspoon chilli powder
350g tomatoes, deseeded and
   finely chopped
15g coriander, leaves removed
   and half chopped, the rest left
   whole for serving
1 lime, halved
sea salt crystals and freshly
   ground black pepper

Crack the eggs into a bowl, then mix in the milk and some salt and pepper with a fork.

Heat the oil in a large frying pan and add the onions, chillies and ginger and cook over a medium heat for about 5 minutes until soft. Stir in the turmeric and chilli powder, add the tomatoes, cover and fry gently for about 5 minutes until thick.

Increase the heat a little, pour in the egg mixture and stir, scraping it from around the edges as it sets. Continue to stir into curds for about 4 minutes until the mixture is no longer loose and it can only just stand in a mound.

Stir in the chopped coriander, squeeze in the lime juice and check the seasoning. Serve right away with the whole coriander leaves scattered over.

batter

Gochujeon with extras

These are a mix of the South Korean *gochujeon* pancake and the Japanese *okonomiyaki* with a few noodles added along the way.

---

enough for 3–4
(makes 10 pancakes)

20g bean thread noodles or dried rice vermicelli noodles, snapped into 2cm lengths (optional)
160g cooked peeled king prawns
3–6 green chillies, deseeded and sliced
4 spring onions, finely sliced
35g plain flour
35g cornflour
3 duck eggs
1 tablespoon fish sauce
1 teaspoon sesame oil
2 tablespoons sunflower oil
4 tablespoons mayonnaise
1 tablespoon sriracha sauce
1 tablespoon toasted sesame seeds

Soak the bean thread noodles in a bowl of boiling water for 20 minutes or until soft. Drain well and set aside. Roughly chop two-thirds of the prawns and put with the noodles and keep the rest aside for serving. Add the chillies and all but a few sliced spring onions.

Put the flours in a bowl and whisk to aerate. Make a well in the middle and crack one egg into it. Whisk so the flour tumbles into the egg, working gradually so that it does not turn lumpy. Add the other eggs, fish sauce, sesame oil and 4 tablespoons water as the batter gets thicker. When it's smooth, stir in the prawn mixture.

Put the sunflower oil in a bowl. Heat a 14cm-base frying pan and smear with a wad of kitchen paper dipped in the oil. Add a small ladleful (or about 2½ tablespoons) of batter. Swirl to coat the pan evenly with the mixture and cook over a low–medium heat for 2 minutes, then flip over and cook for a further 1–2 minutes, pressing down lightly with a piece of kitchen paper. You will have enough batter to make 10 pancakes. Wrap in foil as you cook them and keep warm in a low oven.

Mix the mayonnaise with the sriracha sauce in a small bowl and serve with the reserved prawns and spring onions. Sprinkle over some sesame seeds and eat while hot, with tea.

fried

Herby boxty with crispy egg & pancetta

This Irish dish includes cooked and raw potato for texture. The herb mix is entirely down to personal taste, but I like to throw in a subtle hint of tarragon when it's around. Brown sauce on the side is a must for me, but use what you fancy.

enough for 4

675g King Edward or other
    floury potatoes
2 tablespoons plain spelt flour
½ teaspoon bicarbonate of soda
15g flat-leaf parsley, stems
    trimmed, finely chopped
10g chives, chopped
10g tarragon, leaves removed and
    finely chopped
2 tablespoons natural yogurt
2 small eggs
2 tablespoons extra virgin olive oil
½ teaspoon sea salt crystals
freshly ground black pepper

To serve
2 tablespoons extra virgin olive oil
90–180g thinly sliced raw
    pancetta rashers (depending
    on appetite)
4 medium eggs
brown sauce

Peel all the potatoes. Cut 350g into large pieces and cook in boiling salted water for about 15 minutes or until soft. Put the rest of the potatoes into cold water and set aside.

Put the flour, bicarbonate of soda, salt and freshly ground black pepper in a small bowl and whisk with a fork to aerate.

When the potatoes are tender, drain well in a colander and cover with a few sheets of kitchen paper for a few minutes to dry off. Tip into a large bowl, mash well and spread up the sides of the bowl to cool down quickly.

Meanwhile, finely grate the still-raw potatoes to get long threads. Squeeze all the excess liquid out and add the grated potato to the mash. Add the flour mixture, chopped herbs and the yogurt. Break in the two small eggs and mix well. Whilst still in the bowl, roughly divide into eight mounds.

Put the oven on a low setting – just to keep the boxty warm as you cook them – and line an oven tray with foil. Heat a frying pan, preferably nonstick and large enough to cook four at a time. Add half the olive oil and scoop four portions into the pan, flattening them to roughly 7–8cm rounds. Fry them over a lowish heat for 2–3 minutes on each side until golden and cooked through. Transfer to the oven to keep warm.

When the boxty are cooked, wipe out the pan. Cut the pancetta rashers into 1.5cm pieces with scissors (no need to separate the slices as they do so in the pan), add to the pan and stir-fry over a medium heat for a few minutes until the pieces separate into golden wafers and the fat flows into the pan. Remove with a slotted spoon. Add the olive oil and fry the eggs until the whites turn crispy around the edges and the yolks are still soft.

Serve the boxty with the pancetta and egg and scatter with freshly ground black pepper, some sea salt crystals and a bowl of brown sauce on the side.

fried

Pad kra pao

This version is made with *gai* (chicken) and it's big in Thailand for a super-fast power surge of a brunch or anytime you fancy. It always comes with a fried egg on top, *kài daao*; however, the yolk often arrives hard. To ensure a soft yolk, I have been assured by my son Ben you have to ask for *kài daao daeng* mâi *sòop*, which, translated literally, means 'don't smoke the red bit of the fried egg'! Adding a little store-bought *nam prik* (Thai chilli paste) makes it even better.

enough for 2

90g jasmine rice
½ teaspoon sea salt crystals
2 large skinless chicken breasts
3 short stubby red chillies
6 garlic cloves
2 large eggs
4 tablespoons raw coconut oil
2 tablespoons oyster sauce
2 tablespoons soy sauce
large pinch of organic coconut
   sugar
25g Thai basil, leaves removed
lime wedges, to serve

Put the rice in a sieve and wash until the water is clear. Put in a medium pan with 250ml boiling water and the salt. Bring back to the boil, cover, lower the heat and cook for 12 minutes. Fork over the grains and cover again.

Meanwhile, chop the chicken into small pieces – less than 1cm across – and set aside. Roughly chop the chillies, removing some of the seeds as you go. Bash the garlic to loosen the skins, discard the skins, and cut each clove into three. Pound the chilli and garlic, using a pestle and mortar, to a chunky mixture.

Crack the eggs into separate small bowls. Heat a wok over a high heat and add half the oil. Add one egg, then the other, and fry carefully, basting with hot oil until crispy around the edges but the yolks are still soft. Transfer to a plate and cover with an upturned bowl.

Wipe out the wok with kitchen paper and add the rest of the oil. Heat and add the chilli and garlic and stir-fry for a minute. Add the chicken and stir for a further minute. Add the oyster and soy sauces and the sugar and continue to stir-fry for another minute until the chicken is just tender and cooked through, then fold in most of the basil. Remove from the heat.

Serve the cooked rice in bowls and top with chicken, fried egg and the rest of the basil leaves. Serve with lime wedges for squeezing over the chicken.

in the wok

Egg hoppers with kachumber

The word hopper is a European distortion of the South Indian Tamil word *appam*, meaning pancake, while kachumber is a chopped salad that is popular everywhere in India. As I'm not yet a hopper aficionado I add an egg to my batter – not strictly traditional, but it makes them easier to cook. This recipe will serve 8, but increase the number of eggs and kachumber ingredients to serve more people if you wish as there will be enough batter to make 16 hoppers. The rest of the batter keeps well, covered, in the fridge for 24 hours: enough for another 8 servings using a different filling such as spiced-up chickpeas. Hopper pans are like a wok with two handles and a lid; use a small 20cm wok or a normal frying pan if you can't find one.

enough for 8 / makes 16 hoppers

350ml coconut water, plus extra to
    loosen the mixture, if needed
170g plain flour
80g rice flour
½ teaspoon fast-action dried
    yeast
1 teaspoon sugar
large pinch of turmeric powder
½ teaspoon sea salt crystals
300ml coconut milk
9 large eggs
30g ghee or raw coconut oil,
    for cooking

For the kachumber
50g coriander, leaves removed and
    chopped, a few whole leaves
    reserved to serve
10g mint, leaves removed
    and chopped
2 red chillies, deseeded and
    chopped
3 tomatoes, deseeded and chopped
1cm piece of ginger, scraped and
    finely grated
½ cucumber, deseeded and
    chopped

Heat the coconut water to just lukewarm. Sift the flours into a medium–large bowl and mix in the yeast and sugar. Pour over the lukewarm coconut water and mix to a soft doughy batter. Cover with clingfilm and leave if possible in a warmish place for 1–1½ hours depending on the temperature.

Meanwhile, put all the ingredients for the kachumber (except the whole coriander leaves) in a bowl and mix. Put the aubergine and sweet mango in a bowl and mix with 1 tablespoon water. Put on the table with the kachumber so you are ready for the hot hoppers.

When the batter is ready you will see bubbles under the craggy surface. Whisk in the turmeric and salt followed by the coconut milk and one of the eggs. The batter should be like smooth double cream. Set aside for 5 minutes.

It's easier to make the hoppers if you measure 5 tablespoons of the batter into a small glass (depending on the size of your pan) and have warm serving bowls at the ready for the cooked hoppers. It's a bit of a conveyor-belt production line, ensuring everyone eats a hot hopper with the egg yolk still runny.

Heat the hopper pan or wok over a lowish heat, then add about ¼ teaspoon melted ghee (having it in a pot with a wad of kitchen paper works well for wiping it around). Pour the batter from the glass all in one go, swirling the mixture around the pan to come about 4cm up the sides and slightly thicker on the base until almost wafer-like around the edges.

1 small red onion, finely sliced,
   then each slice cut into
   quarter moons
juice of 1 lime
¼ teaspoon freshly ground cumin
½ teaspoon sea salt crystals

To serve
2 tablespoons aubergine pickle
6 tablespoons sweet mango pickle

Let the hopper cook for 1 minute covered with a lid before breaking an egg
into the middle of the hopper. (While cooking you may need to adjust the
heat up and down for a good result.) Cook for a further 4–5 minutes over
a low heat until the egg white is opaque, the yolk still runny (use the lid
again if you like the yolk slightly more cooked) and the hopper is golden in
patches and easily leaves the edges and base of the pan.

Slide onto a plate and serve right away with the kachumber and pickle
while you make the remaining seven hoppers.

baked

Baked tomatoes & duck eggs with basil

Choose just-ripe heirloom tomatoes for flavour or large salad varieties. Serve with rocket, more basil and plenty of good extra virgin olive oil. You can sit the tomatoes on chunky toast, rubbed with garlic and lots of oil, but I like them just as they are.

enough for 6

6 large tomatoes
3 tablespoons extra virgin olive oil
14 Greek basil sprigs
6 duck eggs
pul biber red pepper flakes
sea salt crystals and freshly ground
   black pepper

Preheat the oven to 200°C/gas mark 6 and line a baking tray with foil.

Without removing the stalk/calix, cut the tops off the tomatoes and set them aside. Scoop the flesh and seeds out of the tomatoes and sit them on the tray. Rub them and their tops with a little of the extra virgin olive oil, place a basil sprig in each, put the tops on and bake in the oven for 8 minutes.

Remove from the oven, put the tops on a plate for later and season the insides of the tomatoes with salt and pepper. Crack one egg at a time into a glass and pop into the tomatoes. Cover the tray with a foil tent, return it to the oven and bake for 15–20 minutes until the whites of the eggs have set and the yolks are still soft (keep checking).

Lift the tomatoes onto a serving dish, spoon over the remaining extra virgin olive oil and scatter with the red pepper flakes and the remaining basil sprigs. Put the lids on the side.

hard & soft boiled

Egg salad with anchovy, caper, olive & pine nuts

This basic combination was used in ancient Roman times – I have revived it because it tastes so good and I'm hooked. I like the double egg use here: a whole soft mollet egg is placed on top of the salad, which includes chopped boiled eggs. It's great served with some crisped flatbreads for scooping and sliced fresh fennel. Without the chopped eggs, the salad would work very well served with Cilbir (see page 41).

enough for 4 as a snack or
2 as a starter

5 wide strips of unwaxed lemon
    rind
50g anchovies in olive oil
extra virgin olive oil, for topping up
6 black olives
25g capers, drained
10g flat-leaf parsley sprigs
5g chives
1 tablespoon white balsamic or
    other white wine vinegar
3 tablespoons pine nuts, toasted
7 medium eggs
freshly ground black pepper

To serve
1 fennel bulb, finely sliced
    lengthways,
crisped flatbreads

Finely chop the lemon rind and put in a serving dish. Drain the oil from the anchovies into a measuring jug and top up to the 75ml mark, if necessary, with extra virgin olive oil. Chop the anchovies into small pieces and put with the lemon. Slice the olives from the stone and chop with the capers; add these to the serving dish. Tear the leaves from the parsley sprigs and chop with the chives, then put in the serving dish with the vinegar, oil from the jug, toasted pine nuts and some black pepper.

Bring a pan of water to the boil and lower the heat before gently adding the eggs – this prevents cracking the shell. Bring back to a simmer and time for 5 minutes. Remove four of the eggs and put into cold water while the other three cook for a further 2 minutes. Shell the four softly cooked eggs carefully and put in a bowl of hot water to keep warm.

When the other three eggs are ready, drain them, put into cold water, then crack and peel right away from the rounded end (they are easier to peel while still slightly hot). Pop into cold water to cool completely. Chop them into the serving dish.

Divide the egg and anchovy mixture between four dishes, top each with a halved, soft mollet egg and scatter with black pepper. Serve with the fennel slices and some crisped flatbreads on the side.

pasta &
steamed yolks

Beetroot tagliatelle with poached yolks & Parmesan

You can buy organic freeze-dried beetroot powder in wholefood shops or online. It gives the tagliatelle its glorious colour as well as a subtle hint of sweetness. If the pasta isn't to be used within a few hours of rolling, fold into nests and open-freeze it overnight, then put in a labelled bag until needed.

enough for 4–6

2 tablespoons extra virgin olive oil
4–6 large egg yolks (allow 1
   per person)

For the pasta
300g '00' pasta flour, plus extra
   for dusting
2 teaspoons beetroot powder
2 medium eggs
3 medium egg yolks
¼ teaspoon sea salt crystals, plus
   1 tablespoon for cooking

To serve
finely grated Parmesan cheese
freshly ground black pepper

To make the pasta, put the flour, beetroot powder and ¼ teaspoon salt in the bowl of a food processor and whizz to aerate. Crack the eggs into a bowl with the separate yolks, break up with a fork and add to the flour. Pulse together until the mixture achieves a couscous-like texture. Turn onto a work surface, knead the dough until it comes together and form into a ball. Flatten a little, then wrap in clingfilm and chill for 30 minutes.

Quarter the dough, roughly shape into a stubby rectangle, using a little flour if need be. Roll out a piece at a time (keeping the rest wrapped) on the widest setting of a pasta roller, fold into three and roll again. Repeat the rolling four times, each time reducing the setting and stretching the dough widthways in between rolls to maintain a width of about 12cm. When the finest setting is reached, cut the length in half and roll once more. Either cut into tagliatelle strips by hand or put through the machine with a tagliatelle attachment fitted. Lay out flat or hang on a rail or the back of a chair until the rest of the pasta has been rolled in the same way.

Fill a large pan three-quarters full with boiling water and bring to a rolling boil. Salt the water and cook the tagliatelle for 2 minutes. Check the pasta is cooked to your liking and drain, put back in the pan and add 1 tablespoon of the oil.

Meanwhile half-fill a frying pan with more boiling water and, over a very low heat, poach the large egg yolks for 1½–2 minutes.

Divide the pasta between serving dishes and top each with a poached egg yolk. Scatter with grated Parmesan and a grinding of black pepper and spoon over the remaining oil.

poached

Poached pheasant eggs with asparagus & celery salt

Pheasant eggs are available only in spring and early summer, so if you cannot find any use bantam eggs, or a small rare breed or guinea fowl eggs. Lovage or parsley could be used for the salt instead of the more common celery. I grow lovage in my garden as it isn't readily available to buy; I love it for its distinctive meaty flavour, even more pungent than celery – so give it a grow!

enough for 4

250g asparagus spears
leaves from a head of organic
    celery
2 teaspoons (minimum) sea
    salt flakes
1 teaspoon white balsamic vinegar
8 pheasant eggs (or bantam or
    guinea fowl)
10g butter

Trim and part-peel the asparagus and put into cold water (this helps to maintain its fresh green colour), drain and set aside. Preheat the oven to 160°C/gas mark 3.

Trim any stems from the celery leaves and put on a baking tray large enough to hold the leaves in a single layer. Bake in the oven for 3–5 minutes until crispy or until the leaves crumble easily but are still bright green – they crisp up more once out of the oven. Leave to cool, then crunch into a powder. Mix in 2 teaspoons salt for every tablespoon of celery. Store in an airtight jar ready to use at any time.

Half-fill a medium pan with boiling water, bring back to the boil and add the vinegar. Break two of the eggs into a cup each and swirl the water in the pan to create a whirlpool. Lower the first egg into the middle followed, by the next, turn off the heat and time for 2 minutes. Check they're cooked by gently lifting with a slotted spoon: if the white needs longer, a further 30 seconds should be enough. Lift the eggs out into a basin of cold water and leave while you cook the remaining six in the same way.

Rinse out the pan and add more boiling water. Drain the asparagus and cook in the water for about 4 minutes until the stems are tender. Drain, toss with the butter and keep warm. Place the eggs in a basin of just-boiled water for about a minute until heated through.

Divide the asparagus between four plates, top each with two eggs and serve with a dusting of the celery salt.

in the pan

Quinoa pancakes with steamed egg, grilled asparagus & tuna

If you wish, you can halve the pancake ingredients given here or keep half the full quantity of batter and use to make a fresh batch of pancakes the next day for breakfast to serve with honeycomb and lemon. The batter improves with keeping overnight in the fridge, but is useable within 30 minutes of making. I prefer non-wheat flour, so this feels right and really nutritious for any meal. Substitute thin green beans or some wilted spinach for asparagus, if you wish.

Makes 12–16 pancakes; other ingredients enough to serve 6

300g thin asparagus spears, trimmed and peeled if wished
1 teaspoon ghee or rapeseed oil, plus extra
6 medium eggs
2 x 160g cans tuna in oil or water, drained
2 cooked beetroot
sea salt crystals and freshly ground black pepper

For the pancakes
150g quinoa flour
100g rice flour
1 teaspoon bicarbonate of soda
1 teaspoon sea salt crystals
400ml cold water
4 medium eggs
75g ghee or rapeseed oil

First make the pancakes. Put the quinoa and rice flour in a large bowl with the bicarbonate of soda and salt. Mix together with a balloon whisk. Measure 400ml cold water into a jug, crack the eggs one at a time into a small bowl and add to the water, whisking to mix.

Make a well in the middle of the flour and add about half the egg mixture. Whisk in the middle, allowing the flour to fall naturally from the edges into the liquid (this avoids lumps). As the mixture thickens add more liquid until all the flour has fallen in and you have a super-smooth batter. Set aside for at least 30 minutes.

Meanwhile, preheat the grill to high and set the shelf about 15cm from the heat. Line a baking sheet with foil and put the asparagus on the foil in an even layer. Add dots of the ghee and put under the grill for a minute. Turn the asparagus to coat with the melted ghee and grill for about a further 2 minutes until cooked to your liking.

Put the tuna in a bowl and slice the beetroot roughly into another bowl. Set aside ready for when the pancakes and eggs are ready.

Heat a 21cm frying pan (preferably one with a clear lid) over a medium heat, then lower right down. Add some hard ghee using the tip of a knife – you want two small knobs to begin with. When it melts, ladle in some batter (you need a ladleful or about 5 tablespoons); you can judge from this first pancake how much is best. It needs to be as thin as possible, so instantly swirl the pan to ensure the batter coats the base right to the edges. Cook for about a minute (it helps to fluctuate the heat between medium and low). Flip the pancake over with a spatula when it is golden underneath. Cook the other side for a further minute or until golden. Slide

onto a warm plate and cover and put into a very low oven until you have
cooked the rest of the pancakes.

Put a pancake at a time into the frying pan over a low heat (no oil required).
Immediately crack an egg onto the pancake and add some asparagus,
cover with a lid and steam-cook for 2 minutes until the egg has just set to
your liking. Transfer to a plate and add some tuna and beetroot and a knob
of ghee to the top and serve right away. Repeat with the other pancakes.

A world of omelettes

pan & oven

Majorcan tortilla

This tortilla is made very differently from most tortillas in as much as you first fluff up the egg whites before adding the yolks and this ensures it's as light as a feather. It gets put in the oven once the underside is cooked in the pan. If you can't find sobrasada, the Majorcan spicy meat paste, use nduja, the hotter Italian version, instead. Skinned and finely chopped chorizo would also work.

enough for 4

2½ tablespoons extra virgin olive oil
1 large onion, finely chopped
4 teaspoons large capers
175g courgettes, sliced into 5mm rounds
75g sobrasada or nduja
6 medium eggs
¼ teaspoon cream of tartar
sea salt crystals

Heat 1 tablespoon of the oil in a 22cm frying pan and fry the onion for about 8 minutes over a low–medium heat until soft and light brown, then tip into a bowl. Wipe out the pan, heat a teaspoon of the oil and fry the capers until crispy; tip onto a plate lined with kitchen paper and put aside for serving.

Preheat the grill to high and put the shelf about 15cm from the heat. Line an oven tray with foil, put the courgette slices on the tray, toss with a teaspoon of the oil and arrange them in a single layer. Grill for about 7 minutes, turning once (they shouldn't overbrown). Mix the onion and the sobrasada in a bowl and fold in the courgettes so as not to break them up.

Preheat the oven to 200°C/gas mark 6. Separate the eggs, putting the whites into a large bowl with the cream of tartar and the yolks in another with a pinch of salt. Using hand-held electric beaters, whisk the whites until the beaters leave a pattern in the foam. Without washing the beaters, whisk the yolks to break them up and mix in some of the whites to loosen the mixture, then fold in the rest to an even colour.

Heat the rest of the oil in the wiped-out frying pan over a medium heat. When the oil is just hot, ensure the pan is evenly coated and pour in the egg mixture, immediately lowering the heat. Dot over the courgette and sobrasada mixture and watch the edges of the tortilla closely. When it starts to separate a little (use a palette knife to ease the edges gently away from the pan) and is feeling firmer around the edges, put in the hot oven (if the pan handle isn't ovenproof, wrap it in thick foil) and cook for 10–12 minutes until puffed and golden. It should be just set in the middle although it will still feel a little wobbly. Slide onto a board with the help of a palette knife and scatter with the crispy capers.

in the pan

Bun Cha with omelette noodles

I've fiddled with this dish over the years, as it's both my sons' favourite Vietnamese street food, next in line to the delicious Pho. Bun Cha infers smoky charcoal-grilled pork with rice noodles but this is my latest interpretation. If your butcher will freshly grind your mince from fatty belly pork, all the better!

enough for 4

2 tablespoons golden caster sugar
2 tablespoons fish sauce
350g pork mince
2 garlic cloves, crushed to a paste
   with a few sea salt crystals
1 teaspoon freshly ground black
   pepper
1 medium egg
1 tablespoon raw coconut oil,
   for frying

For the omelette noodles
4 large eggs
½ teaspoon sesame oil
1 teaspoon light soy sauce
2 teaspoons fish sauce
¼ teaspoon chilli flakes, pounded
   to a powder
1 tablespoon raw coconut oil

For the sauce
3 tablespoons fish sauce
1 tablespoon golden caster sugar
1 large chilli, deseeded and finely
   chopped
2 garlic cloves, crushed to a paste
   with a few sea salt crystals
juice of 1 lime

To serve
100g beansprouts, roots trimmed
15g sweet Thai basil (or ordinary)
10g mint and coriander leaves
1 small mango, peeled and sliced
   into wedges
1 lime, cut into wedges

Put the sugar in a small pan with 2 tablespoons water over a low heat. As soon as the sugar dissolves increase the heat and cook to a rich caramel. Remove from the heat and carefully add 1 tablespoon water mixed with the fish sauce. Set aside to get cold.

Put the mince in a bowl with the garlic, pepper, cold caramel and egg. Mix well and leave to marinate and chill while preparing the rest.

Put all the ingredients for the omelette noodles in a bowl with 1 tablespoon water. Whisk to combine then set aside.

To make the sauce, put all the ingredients in a bowl with 2 tablespoons water and mix well – put back over the heat if you need to dissolve it.

Form the mince mixture into 14 patties and put on a plate, then melt the coconut oil and spoon over to cover all sides. Preheat a griddle pan over a high heat and cook for 3 minutes on each side, until done. Transfer to a plate and cover with foil to keep warm.

Heat a 20cm frying pan over a medium–high heat and swirl in a little of the oil. Reduce the heat and ladle in about a quarter of the omelette noodle mixture, swirling to coat the base of the pan evenly. When the mixture sets, after about 2 minutes, and it flips easily, turn it to cook the other side for about a minute. Roll into a cigar shape and wrap in foil while you make another three. When the omelettes are all cooked, slice them into thin noodles.

Serve the noodles with the pork patties, beansprouts, herb leaves, mango slices, lime wedges and sauce.

in the pan

Prawn & chilli omelette with nam jim dressing

I buy prawns in the shell from my favourite fishmonger and peel them as soon as I get home. They are usually fresher and cheaper that way, otherwise buy them in packs ready prepared. I squeeze over the lime juice right away and they sit happily in the fridge for a few hours. I drain and salt them just before cooking.

enough for 3

500g large raw prawns, peeled or 250g ready prepared
juice of 1 lime
sea salt crystals
1 tablespoon sunflower oil
20g Thai basil, leaves removed
small handful of micro coriander and red amaranth or coriander leaves, to serve

For the chilli omelettes
4 large eggs
1 garlic clove, crushed to a paste
½ teaspoon toasted sesame oil
1½ teaspoons light soy sauce
4 teaspoons sweet chilli dipping sauce
1 tablespoon sunflower oil

For the nam jim
2 tablespoons organic coconut sugar
2 garlic cloves, finely chopped
2cm piece of ginger, scraped and grated
2 small Thai or 1 small banana shallots, finely chopped
3 tablespoons fish sauce
10g coriander sprigs, leaves removed and roughly chopped
juice of 2 large limes – you need about 50ml of juice
4 tablespoons sweet chilli dipping sauce
1 long red chilli, deseeded and finely chopped

To make the nam jim, put all the ingredients in a mini processor and whizz to combine to a chunky sauce or pound them in a pestle and mortar. To prepare the prawns, pour over the lime juice, cover and set aside. Preheat the oven to low and put in a plate to warm up.

Crack the eggs into a measuring jug and whisk with 1 tablespoon water. Add the garlic, sesame oil, soy sauce and chilli dipping sauce and mix together. Heat a 20cm-base frying pan over a medium heat and add a little of the oil, spreading it around the pan with kitchen paper so it doesn't puddle. Ladle in a sixth of the omelette mixture and swirl the pan to coat the base evenly then turn down the heat. Let it gently set and turn golden on the base for about 1 minute. Fold it into four quarters in the pan so the golden underside is on the outside and put on the warm plate in the oven. Repeat with the rest of the mixture to make five more omelettes.

Drain the prawns, pat with kitchen paper and sprinkle with a little salt. Heat the oil in a large wok and lift all the prawns into it with a slotted spoon. Let them sear on one side until pink, then stir-fry them for a few minutes until cooked through and evenly pink. Add the basil leaves and stir to wilt them into the prawns.

Serve a couple of omelettes on each plate, some of the prawns on top and a spoon or two of nam jim. Scatter with the micro coriander and red amaranth and serve while hot.

New potato, leek & goat's cheese frittata with a touch of chilli

Spring-like and fresh-tasting, this dish uses new potatoes and young tender leeks; if you can find wild garlic leaves in farmers' markets or in the wild in early spring, slice in a few. Add a flash of chilli for colour and heat only if you want – a thing I'm all in favour of.

enough for 6

350g new potatoes, scrubbed
250g young leeks
25g butter
2 tablespoons extra virgin olive oil
2 tablespoons chopped chives
1 teaspoon pul biber red pepper
    flakes
6 large eggs
150g firm goat's cheese, crumbled
    (leave the rind on)
sea salt crystals and freshly
    ground black pepper

Cook the potatoes in a pan of boiling salted water for 10–20 minutes. Drain well and, when they are cool enough to handle, peel off the papery skin, if you wish. Meanwhile, slice the leeks, wash well and leave to drain in a colander. Cut the potatoes into slices about 0.5cm thick and set aside.

Heat a frying pan of about 23cm diameter over a medium heat and add the butter, oil and leeks. Stir, lower the heat a little and leave to wilt and soften for about 5 minutes, stirring often so the leeks don't brown. Stir in the potatoes, chives and red pepper flakes and turn off the heat.

Crack the eggs into a bowl and whisk with a fork. Preheat the grill to medium and set the shelf about 20cm from the heat. Turn the heat under the pan back on to low, and add the eggs, salt and pepper, moving the mixture around in the pan so it's evenly mixed with some of the solids on the top. Cook for about 5 minutes until just starting to firm up a little around the edges and slightly bubbling in the middle. Leave over a very low heat for a few more minutes. Scatter the cheese on the top and pop under the grill for about 3 minutes until puffed at the edges and set in the middle. (If your pan handle is not ovenproof, wrap it in foil.)

Leave to cool a little before serving dusted with a few more red pepper flakes, if you wish.

Classic rolled omelette with herbs

The perfect rolled omelette is simplicity itself, taking mere seconds to cook, and it can be made to your taste, either slightly runny or firm. It will continue to cook once folded and on the plate, so if softness is what you want roll it onto your plate sooner rather than later. I add tiny cubes of the butter to the mix, which makes it creamier without making it heavy, but you could leave this out. A just-warm plate is essential, I think, and buttered toast.

enough for 1

3 medium eggs
15g butter or ½ teaspoon
    rapeseed oil
1 tablespoon finely chopped
    fresh herbs (use a mixture like
    parsley, oregano and chives)
sea salt crystals and freshly
    ground black pepper
freshly grated Parmesan cheese,
    to serve (optional)

Crack the eggs into a shallow dish (it's easier for mixing them lightly) and add seasoning. Cut 10g of the butter (if using) into tiny cubes and add, along with the chopped herbs. Beat the eggs lightly with a fork just to break up the yolks into the whites.

Warm a 20cm-base frying pan over a medium–high heat and add the rest of the butter. As soon as it foams (don't let it turn golden) swirl the pan to coat the base evenly with the butter and pour in the egg mixture. Pass the flat side of the fork under the eggs, as quickly as you can, exposing as much of the mixture as possible to the hot pan.

Pull in the sides of the omelette in a few places and tilt the pan so the soft egg runs into the spaces. When it is cooked to your liking, with the help of the fork, fold one edge into the middle then fold the other edge over the top and slide it onto a warm plate. Scatter with Parmesan.

Egg-white omelette
– a power breakfast

enough for 1

Take three large egg whites, put into a jar, add seasoning and shake the jar to mix well. Heat a pan as for the omelette above and add ½ teaspoon rapeseed oil. Swirl it around the base of the pan, tip in the whites and cook as above.

in the pan

Kaygana with nuts & cheese

Found all over Turkey and also Crete, this dates back to the Ottoman Empire. Kaygana is where omelette meets pancake with its addition of a little fine cornmeal. It is as delicious served with jam or fruit compote as its many savoury versions. You could cut each one in half to serve 4 as a snack.

enough for 2–4

2 tablespoons fine cornmeal
4 tablespoons live yogurt
3 medium eggs
8 anchovy fillets in olive oil,
    drained and finely chopped
10g bunch flat-leaf parsley, leaves
    removed and chopped
15g butter
75g feta cheese
1 tablespoon shelled and chopped
    pistachios
freshly ground black pepper
sumac, for dusting (optional)
extra virgin olive oil, to serve

Put the cornmeal in a bowl and mix in the yogurt. Crack in the eggs, add 2 tablespoons water and whisk with a fork, then stir in the anchovies and parsley.

Heat a 20cm frying pan, melt half the butter and pour in half the mixture. After a second or two, swirl the pan to coat the base evenly. After about 1½ minutes or when the mixture is set on the underside, flip over a third and then bring the opposite side over and jiggle onto a plate. Crumble over half the feta, scatter with half the nuts, dust with pepper and sumac (if using) and drizzle with extra virgin olive oil to serve. Make the other kaygana in the same way.

Oven omelette for a small crowd

This easy way to feed a few people nonchalantly for Sunday brunch and feel good about it. When the omelette is cooked and ready, plonk the oven tin in the middle of the table with lots of forks and small plates and let everyone dive in. Have lots of bread too, slathered with lashings of salty butter, and make plenty of good coffee. This is influenced by the eggah and the kuku (see pages 111 and 119), both of which traditionally can be cooked either in the oven or on the hob and finished under a grill.

enough for 5–6

butter, for greasing
250g cherry tomatoes on the vine
200g button chestnut mushrooms
140g diced pancetta or lardons
2 tablespoons extra virgin olive oil
75g mangetout
10 medium eggs
3 tablespoons pitted Kalamata
    olives
4 tablespoons freshly grated
    Parmesan cheese, plus extra
    to serve
sea salt crystals and freshly
    ground black pepper

Preheat the oven to 200°C/fan 180°C/gas mark 6. Grease an oven tin about 19 x 22cm.

Strip the tomatoes from the vine and put them in the tin with the mushrooms and diced pancetta, toss with the oil and cook in the oven for 15 minutes.

Meanwhile, pile a few mangetout together at a time and shred them into three lengths. Blanch for 2 minutes in boiling salted water, drain and refresh under the cold tap. Crack the eggs into a bowl and break up just a little with a fork so the yolks are still yellow pieces within the whites, add a little salt.

Remove the tin from the oven, pour over the eggs, scatter with the mangetout and olives, grind over some black pepper, then add the grated Parmesan in patches. Return the tin to the oven for 10–12 minutes until the omelette is set and puffy at the edges.

in the pan &
under the grill

A Roman frittata

I ate this on a visit to Rome just as the tiny purple artichokes came into season. They were deep-fried then added to the frittata but, for ease and speed, I use good-quality canned or jarred artichoke hearts or a few picked up from the deli counter. Frozen broad beans are a good substitute when fresh ones aren't about, except it's nicer if you pop them out of their grey skins to show off their bright green colour.

enough for 4

6 canned or jarred artichokes, with a little stem if possible, drained well and halved lengthways
5 duck eggs
4 tablespoons full-fat milk
100g shelled broad beans
2 tablespoons extra virgin olive oil
4 spring onions, finely sliced
25g Parmesan cheese, grated
5g sprigs marjoram or oregano, leaves removed and chopped
sea salt crystals and freshly ground black pepper

Drain the artichokes on some kitchen paper. Crack the eggs into a bowl, add the milk and whisk with a fork. Cook the broad beans in a pan of boiling salted water for 3 minutes, drain, refresh in cold water and drain again (at this point you can pop them out of the skins if you wish).

Heat half the oil in a frying pan and fry the artichokes cut-side down until lightly golden, then add the spring onions and heat, briefly, just to wilt. Lift the vegetables out with a slotted spoon onto a plate. Mix the Parmesan, marjoram and seasoning into the eggs.

Preheat the grill to medium and put the shelf in the middle. Wipe out the pan, heat the rest of the oil over a medium heat and pour in the egg mixture. When the mixture starts to set around the edge, move it slightly in parts around the edge and tilt the pan so any runny egg flows into the spaces. When puffs of steam start to appear in the middle but the egg is still runny, scatter over the broad beans and the artichokes. Put under the grill (if your pan has a handle that might melt, wrap it in foil) for about 4 minutes until puffy around the edge and set in the middle. Turn the grill to high and cook for a further minute.

Salt cod & spinach tortilla

I like to salt my own fish overnight so it's soft and doesn't require soaking before use, unlike bacalao – the salted and dried cod used in Spain and Portugal. Of course, if you have no time for this just salt the fish for as long as you can. I like to substitute sweet potato for the traditional waxy potato. This is my favourite pincho to munch on with a few chatos – small shots of red wine.

enough for 6 as a pincho
with drinks

150g cod or haddock loin or
    skinned fillet
6 tablespoons extra virgin olive oil
1 medium onion, finely chopped
250g sweet potatoes, peeled and
    thinly sliced
6 large eggs
250g spinach
sea salt crystals and freshly
    ground black pepper

Sprinkle a teaspoon of sea salt crystals on each side of the fish, place in a non-reactive dish, cover and leave in the fridge overnight (if longer, soak in cold water for 15 minutes). Rinse the salt off the fish under the cold tap, put the fish in a small pan and just cover with water. Bring to a gentle simmer, then immediately turn off the heat and leave for 5–8 minutes; the fish only needs to flake when persuaded, so don't overcook. Drain well, flake onto a plate and put aside.

Heat 5 tablespoons of the oil in a 20cm frying pan and add the onion and potatoes. Cover and fry for 10–15 minutes until soft but still pale (the onion may colour a tiny bit). Turn them frequently to stop them sticking and remove the pan from the heat when done.

Meanwhile, crack the eggs into a bowl, whisk and add pepper along with the flaked fish.

Put the spinach in a large bowl and pour over boiling water to wilt the leaves for about a minute. Drain and refresh under cold water. Squeeze out as much moisture as possible and add to the egg mixture.

Reheat the pan of onion and potato over a low heat and pour in the egg mixture, moving it with a spatula to get the solid pieces evenly distributed throughout. When the mixture starts to set around the edge, move it slightly in parts on the edge and tilt the pan so any runny egg flows into the spaces.

When the bottom is golden and the top looks just about set, put a plate over the pan and turn it upside down onto the plate. Wipe out the pan, then add the rest of the oil to heat. Slide the tortilla back in, cooked-side up, and continue to cook for 2 minutes until pale golden in parts and set. Slide it onto a plate and leave for 5 minutes before cutting into small pieces.

souffléd

Souffléd omelette with Camembert & persillade

You can forgo the persillade if you wish and just go with the salad leaves and herbs, but it's so good with the puffy omelette you have to give it a try if you have time. You can use Brie or Epoisses instead of Camembert, if you like.

enough for 2

3 medium egg whites
pinch of cream of tartar
2 medium egg yolks
¼ teaspoon sea salt crystals
1 teaspoon olive oil
½ a ripe Camembert cheese,
  sliced vertically into 4
salad, micro leaves or herbs,
  to serve

For the persillade
20g flat-leaf parsley, leaves
  removed and finely chopped
2 garlic cloves, crushed to a paste
  with a few sea salt crystals
2 tablespoons extra virgin olive oil

Mix the persillade ingredients together and set aside.

Preheat the oven to 150°C/ gas mark 3. Put the egg whites and cream of tartar in a bowl and use hand-held electric beaters to whisk until firm and the beaters leave a pattern in the foam. Put the yolks and salt in a large bowl and, without washing the beaters, whisk until smooth. Fold through the egg whites to an even colour.

Heat half the oil in a 20–22cm frying pan over a low–medium heat and wipe it around the base with kitchen paper. Pour in half the egg mixture and jiggle the frothy mixture to coat the base of the pan evenly. Cook for 3–3½ minutes until golden on the underside and puffy and almost set on the top. Lay half the camembert slices on one half of the omelette and cook for a further minute. Fold over the other half to make a half-moon. Slide onto a plate and pop in the oven to keep warm while you cook the next one.

Serve with the persillade and scatter with salad, micro leaves or herbs.

Golden yolk & tomato salsa omelette

You could use extra chopped herbs instead of the tomato salsa or just chopped raw tomato.

enough for 2 as a snack or 1 as a meal

4 medium eggs
1 teaspoon butter
10g chunk of Parmesan cheese
parsley or coriander leaves, for
    scattering
sea salt crystals and freshly
    ground black pepper

For the salsa
2 plum tomatoes, deseeded and
    chopped
1 small red onion, finely chopped
10g flat-leaf parsley, leaves
    removed and chopped
1 teaspoon pul biber red pepper
    flakes
juice of ½ lime

To make the salsa, combine the ingredients in a bowl and put aside.

Separate two of the eggs, putting the yolks in two small separate bowls and set aside. Crack the other two eggs into a bowl, and use a fork to whisk in the separated whites and seasoning a little, without breaking the whole eggs up too much.

Heat a 20–22cm frying pan and add the butter. When it fizzes, tilt the pan so the base gets an even coating of butter and pour in the egg mixture. When the mixture starts to set around the edge move it inwards slightly in areas around the edge and tilt the pan so any runny egg flows into the spaces created.

Lower the heat and spoon over some salsa, add a yolk to each half of the omelette, cover the pan and cook for about 2 minutes until just set. Grate over some Parmesan and scatter with the herbs. Cut in half and slide onto two warm plates; serve any leftover salsa alongside.

pan & oven

Omelette au gratin

These greens-and-cheese-filled omelettes are rolled and tucked into a baking dish cut-side up and finished off with a sprinkling of extra Comté, a sweet nutty melting cheese. The pink peppercorns give their own unique flavour, so use black pepper instead if you're not sure about it. The tomato vinaigrette (see page 36) would be perfect with this along with a salad.

enough for 4

4 teaspoons rapeseed oil, plus
    extra for greasing
175g chard or spinach, thick
    stems removed
8 medium eggs
1 teaspoon pink peppercorns,
    roughly crushed, or freshly
    ground black pepper
200g Comté or Emmental cheese,
    finely grated
small pinch of sea salt crystals

To serve
tomato vinaigrette (see page 36,
    optional)
salad leaves

Preheat the oven to 220°C/ gas mark 7 and grease a 17cm x 22cm ovenproof dish.

Put the chard leaves in a large pan and pour over boiling water from the kettle. Bring back to the boil, drain and refresh under the cold tap until cold. Squeeze as much excess moisture out of the leaves as possible.

Crack the eggs into a measuring jug, add the pink peppercorns and a small pinch of salt, then lightly break up with a fork. Heat ½ teaspoon of the oil in a 20cm-base pan over a medium–low heat. Pour in around an eighth of the mixture and swirl the pan to coat the base evenly. Cook for 1½ minutes, shaking the pan to loosen the omelette, and slide onto a board. Continue making another seven in the same way.

While they cook, start to fill the cooked omelettes. Lay some flattened-out chard leaves over the surface, scatter some of the cheese over the top and roll loosely. Line up all the rolls and use a sharp knife to cut about 1cm off the ends that are less filled. Then cut each trimmed omelette roll into four.

Put the cut-off trimmings in the base of the oven dish and stand the filled rolls cut-side up on top, packing them in so they don't fall over. Scatter over a little cheese and bake in the oven for 8 minutes until its melted.

in the pan &
under the grill

The chicken, the aubergine & the eggah

Don't expect this Arabian eggah to be light and fluffy like an omelette. In fact it's more like a savoury cake, solid with ingredients. The Moorish conquest of Spain links it to the Spanish tortilla, although the origins of the tortilla couldn't be more confusing: exactly who did introduce it to whom? You can cover and bake your eggah in the oven at 160°C/gas mark 3 for 35 minutes if you wish, but the dish is more commonly covered and cooked slowly over a very gentle heat. Serve hot with spinach or cold liberally strewn with herbs and micro leaves.

enough for 4–6

2 boneless chicken breasts
5 tablespoons extra virgin olive oil, plus extra for greasing
1 large onion, finely chopped
1 large (400g) aubergine, trimmed and cut into roughly 1cm cubes
¾ teaspoon ground cinnamon
½ teaspoon pul biber red pepper flakes
½ teaspoon freshly ground black pepper
3 tablespoons lightly toasted pine nuts
6 large eggs
2 teaspoons ghee
sea salt crystals

Preheat the oven to 190°C/gas mark 5 and line a baking tray with foil.

Put the chicken on the tray, season well and rub with 1 tablespoon of the oil. Bake for 20 minutes. Cut into roughly 1cm pieces and set aside.

Meanwhile, heat another tablespoon of the oil in a frying pan and cook the onion for about 5 minutes until soft and golden. Set aside.

Heat a wok over a high heat, add the rest of the oil and the aubergine cubes and stir-fry (they will look dry for a time but don't be tempted to add more oil) until the oil starts to ooze out, then continue to fry until soft and golden – about 7 minutes in total.

Remove from the heat, add the onion and chicken with the cinnamon, red pepper flakes, black pepper, a pinch of salt and the pine nuts and stir together well. Crack the eggs into a large bowl, whisk with a pinch of salt, then stir in the contents of the wok a little at a time.

Melt the ghee in a 20cm heavy-based frying pan and pour in the mixture, cover with a sheet of greased foil and cook gently over a very low heat for 20 minutes. Remove the foil and pop under a hot grill for a few minutes until the top looks slightly golden and a little puffy. Alternatively, if cooking in the oven (see introduction, above) remove the foil for the last 5 minutes to firm up the middle.

souffléd

Mini cloud loaves

This incredibly popular health fad has become a firm favourite with me. I have tried it in all forms but love it as a mini loaf shape which I slice in half and use to make a flour-free bacon sandwich with sliced tomato and watercress – it's delicious. Make in a larger tin if you wish or in single round tins. Try it halved and toasted too.

enough for 6

butter, for greasing
3 large eggs
¼ teaspoon cream of tartar
45g cream cheese
¼ teaspoon turmeric powder
pinch of sea salt crystals

To serve
grilled streaky bacon
sliced tomato
watercress

Preheat the oven to 180°C/gas mark 4. Grease six mini loaf tins with butter and line the bases with non-stick baking paper.

Separate the eggs, putting the whites in a large bowl and the yolks in a medium bowl.

Add the cream of tartar to the bowl with the whites and the cream cheese, turmeric and salt to the bowl with the yolks. Use hand-held electric beaters to whisk the whites until they are firm enough to make patterns in the mixture. Without washing the beaters, whisk the yolk mixture for a few minutes until smooth.

Fold the yolk mixture gradually into the whites to get an even colour, keeping the volume. Spoon the mixture into the prepared mini loaf tins, place on a baking sheet and bake in the oven for 20 minutes, turning the tray front to back half-way through. Serve sliced in half horizontally and pack with bacon, tomato and watercress.

in the oven

Trout & lemon strata

This is omelette meets bread pudding and is a very satisfying supper dish. You could use three times the quantity of cheese instead of the trout. It is best if you can leave the made up strata overnight in the fridge so the bread soaks up the eggy mixture, but bring to room temperature for about 20 minutes before cooking otherwise it will need longer in the oven to set.

enough for 8

250g chunky trout or salmon
   fillets, skinned
finely grated zest of 1 lemon
200g spinach
about 175g crusty French
   baguette, cut into 2–3cm cubes
8 large eggs
150ml double cream
300ml full-fat milk
sea salt crystals and freshly
   ground black pepper

Cut the trout into 2cm cubes and put into an ovenproof china dish about 18 x 32cm. Scatter with the lemon zest and a sprinkling of salt. Put the spinach in a bowl, pour over boiling water and leave for 2 minutes to wilt, then drain well. Squeeze as much liquid out as you can, roughly chop and scatter over the trout. Add the bread cubes to the mixture.

Crack the eggs into a bowl and break them up with a balloon whisk. Add the cream, milk and seasoning, then whisk well until smooth. Pour over the mixture in the dish and toss everything together until evenly mixed. Cover with clingfilm and chill for 4 hours or up to 24 hours.

Remove the strata from the fridge 20 minutes to an hour before cooking. Preheat the oven to 180°C/gas mark 4. Bake the strata for 25 minutes until puffed and golden.

in the oven

Cauliflower cheese frittata pots with hot gremolata

This can always be reheated if you protect the whole dish in a foil parcel – place in a medium oven and heat for 8 minutes. I like this served with crispy streaky bacon for a quick lunch with some really tasty salad leaves, simply dressed.

enough for 4

butter, for greasing
1 large cauliflower (about 800g)
5 large eggs
150ml double cream
200g mature Cheddar cheese,
   finely grated
sea salt crystals and freshly
   ground black pepper

For the hot gremolata
20g flat-leaf parsley
1 unwaxed lemon
2 garlic cloves, crushed
2 tablespoons extra virgin olive oil
pinch of pul biber red pepper
   flakes or chilli flakes

Preheat the oven to 200°C/gas mark 6. Grease 4 x 350ml ovenproof dishes. Cut the stems from the cauliflower and break into small florets. Slice the stems and put them and the florets in a medium pan with a large pinch of salt. Pour boiling water over the cauliflower to cover and cook on a medium heat for 5 minutes. Drain well.

Crack the eggs into a large bowl, add the cream and whisk with a pinch of salt and black pepper. Fold in the cheese and the drained cauliflower. Pile the mixture into the four greased dishes and bake in the oven for 22 minutes until golden.

Meanwhile, make the gremolata. Strip the leaves off the parsley and finely chop. Using a vegetable peeler, slice thin strips of zest off the lemon and finely chop. Put in a small frying pan with the parsley, garlic and the olive oil, fry over a medium heat for a few minutes and add the chilli. Tip onto a plate lined with kitchen paper.

When the cauliflower cheese frittata pots are ready, take to the table and serve with the hot gremolata in small pots to scatter over the tops.

in the pan

Nasi goreng

The Indonesian nasi goreng is the fried rice dish with lots of tasty bits (such as plenty of sliced omelette) that every cook makes their own, but the method is always the same. Cold rice is the secret to good fried rice, so plan to cook it ahead. If that fails, speed up the process by spreading the hot rice in a cold deep roasting tin, then half-submerge this in a sink of cold water to cool it quickly.

enough for 4–6

225g basmati rice
1 large lime
400g skinless chicken breast
2 tablespoons light soy sauce
200g raw prawns, peeled and
    deveined
1 teaspoon red chilli flakes
1 medium onion, roughly chopped
3 garlic cloves, roughly chopped
½ teaspoon dried shrimp paste
½ teaspoon chilli paste
4 medium eggs
raw coconut oil, for frying
1 large bunch spring onions,
    trimmed and finely sliced
    diagonally
sea salt crystals and freshly
    ground black pepper

To serve
sliced red chillies
sliced cucumber
crispy fried shallots
lettuce wedges

Put the rice in a bowl with 1 teaspoon salt, cover with water and leave for 30 minutes. Rinse and put in a pan with 450ml water and the juice of half the lime. Bring to the boil, lower the heat, cover and cook for 8 minutes until tender. Drain and spread on a tray and cool completely.

When the rice is cold, cut the chicken into thin slices and put in a bowl with 1 tablespoon of the soy sauce. Put the prawns in another bowl with the rest of the lime juice and the chilli flakes. Put the onion, garlic, shrimp and chilli pastes in a mini processor with 2 teaspoons water and whizz to a paste (or use a pestle and mortar).

Crack the eggs into a bowl and whisk with the remaining soy sauce, 3 tablespoons water and some pepper. Heat a 20–22cm-base frying pan and add a little oil, spreading it around the pan with kitchen paper. Lower the heat and ladle in about a sixth of the omelette mixture, swirling to coat the base evenly. Let it gently set and colour on the base for about 1½ minutes. Slide the omelette onto a plate, cover with foil and keep it warm in a very low oven. Make the other five omelettes in the same way.

Heat a large wok, add 1 tablespoon oil and stir-fry the spring onions for a few seconds to wilt, then lift onto a plate. Add a little more oil and stir-fry the chicken for a few minutes; add the prawns and stir-fry for a further 2 minutes, then tip onto the plate with the spring onions.

Heat a little more oil and stir-fry the onion paste for 3 minutes, taking care not to burn it. Add the cold rice and stir-fry until hot. Add the chicken and prawns and toss to combine. Roll up the omelettes, slice into 1cm strips and fold most of them into the rice, reserving the rest along with the listed extra ingredients for serving.

Kuku sabzi

A Persian herby omelette is usually served at New Year as a symbol of rebirth and fertility. Sabzi is Farsi for herbs and kuku is an egg-based dish. It can be cooked on the hob covered with a lid or in the oven covered with a loose tent of foil so the prawns cook in the steam that's created. I like to add prawns although they're not part of a traditional Persian kuku. For a more substantial meal I, serve with a few small baked potatoes.

enough for 6–8

15g butter, plus extra for greasing
12 large raw prawns, peeled but with tails intact
2 tablespoons olive oil
1 fennel bulb with plenty of green fronds, quartered and finely sliced
125g (about 2) small leeks, quartered then roughly chopped
6 large eggs
10g flat-leaf parsley sprigs, leaves removed and finely chopped
5g mint sprigs, leaves removed and finely chopped
10g oregano sprigs, leaves removed and chopped
5g fennel herb, if available
½ teaspoon sea salt crystals
½ teaspoon freshly ground black pepper

Preheat the oven to 190°C/gas mark 5. Lightly grease a baking dish or oven tin about 22 x 17cm or a 18cm ovenproof frying pan. Cut down the back of each prawn to 'butterfly' and remove the dark vein if there is one. Leave the tail shells intact so the prawns can stand upright. Set aside.

Put the butter and oil in a frying pan and cook the fennel bulb (keeping the fronds for serving) over a medium heat for 3 minutes. Add the leeks and cook for 5 minutes, continuing to stir so they don't scorch. Put the eggs in a bowl and whisk with a fork to break up, add the herbs, then cooked fennel and leeks, salt and pepper.

Pour into the dish and sit the prawns with their tails upright in the mixture. Cover carefully with a tent of foil and bake in the oven for 25–35 minutes. Uncover and carry on cooking for a further 5 minutes until just firm.
Let it rest for 5 minutes, scatter over the fronds kept from the fennel tops and serve.

Suppers
&
comforts

scrambled

Egg-fried buckwheat with peas, mangetout & bacon

Buckwheat, being a gluten-free seed, not wheat, is a handy thing to use if avoiding grains, as many people are for a variety of good reasons. I always loved egg-fried rice so decided to give raw organic buckwheat a go instead. Kasha is toasted buckwheat, but I like to use raw organic buckwheat – soaked for 7 hours for optimum goodness – and it takes no time to cook. I cook the buckwheat separately to the eggs in a kind of scramble-meets-omelette affair. If preferred, use small, cooked peeled cooked prawns instead of bacon.

enough for 4–6

150g raw organic buckwheat, soaked no more than 7 hours in lots of cold water
3 tablespoons extra virgin olive oil
100g back bacon, chopped, or small cooked peeled prawns
4 medium eggs
75g mangetout, shredded
1 long red chilli, deseeded and finely chopped
2cm piece of ginger, scraped and sliced thinly, then cut into thin strands
1 bunch spring onions, trimmed and thinly sliced into rounds
100g petits pois
3 tablespoons light soy sauce, plus extra to serve
small bunch of coriander, leaves removed and chopped if large
sea salt crystals and freshly ground black pepper

Drain and rinse the soaked buckwheat. Put in a pan with enough cold water to cover by 2cm. Bring gently to a simmer and cook for about 5–10 minutes. Check often, because it stays looking firm – it should be just soft when done. Drain well and spread it on a baking tray so that it dries as it cools.

Heat 1 tablespoon of the oil in a large frying pan and fry the bacon pieces until golden. Lift onto a plate leaving the oil in the pan. Crack the eggs into a bowl, season and whisk with a fork. Heat the frying pan, pour in the eggs and let them set a little for a minute. Bring all the edges into the middle of the pan and cook for a further minute, scrambling the eggs by moving the mixture around the pan until it starts to firm up – you don't want a wet scramble. Tip onto the plate with the bacon and clean out the frying pan.

Blanch the shredded mangetout in a small pan of boiling salted water for 1 minute, drain and put with the eggs and bacon.

Add the rest of the oil to the frying pan and add the chillies and ginger. Fry for 1 minute then add the spring onions and, after 30 seconds, the buckwheat. Stir-fry for 4 minutes until hot, add the peas, bacon, egg and mangetout along with the soy sauce and mix together well. Check for seasoning and add more soy sauce to taste and sprinkle with the coriander to serve.

soft boiled

A kind of Florentine with mollet eggs

From the French *molle*, meaning 'soft', mollet eggs have a runny yolk and a white firm enough to peel easily so the whole egg can be put on the plate hot and unbroken. I use smoked haddock instead of ham in my cheat's version of eggs Florentine, which classically has a mornay sauce and poached eggs – my combo uses mollet eggs and reduced double cream.

enough for 2

300g smoked haddock fillet
150ml double cream
2 large eggs
small knob of butter, plus extra
   for greasing
100g baby leaf spinach
sea salt crystals and freshly
   ground black pepper

Cut the haddock in half across and put in a pan with enough cold water just to cover. Place over a medium heat and as soon as it boils lower the heat and time 3 minutes. Lift onto a plate, leaving as much liquid behind as possible. Set aside to cool.

Meanwhile, put the cream in a small pan and bring to a simmer, lower the heat right down and leave for 5 minutes to thicken (make sure it doesn't burn on the bottom).

Add more water to what remains in the fish cooking pan and bring back to the boil. Then, off the heat (so they don't crack), add the eggs, return to the heat and cook for 5 minutes on a lowered heat. Drain, refresh briefly in cold water, carefully crack and peel from the rounded end and set aside.

Rinse out the pan and add a knob of butter and the spinach with a pinch of salt. Cover and cook over a medium heat for a minute or so until just wilted. Drain well.

Preheat the grill to high and place a shelf 15cm away from the heat. Grease two gratin-style 12–14cm dishes with sides 3cm-deep (or use one larger dish). Flake the fish off the skin, removing any stray bones as you do, and add to the spinach. Divide between the dishes and place a mollet egg in the middle of each one, pour the cream over and around the egg and grind over some pepper. Grill for 1½–2 minutes until speckled golden.

pasta & boiled

Fresh duck egg noodles with boiled eggs, prawns & peanut dressing

Try using plain spelt flour instead of the classic tipo '00' Italian flour and whizz it in a processor to make it finer before using.

enough for 4

4 medium eggs
6 spring onions, thinly shredded lengthways, soaked in cold water
2 tablespoons sunflower oil
1 fennel bulb, trimmed and thinly sliced
1 medium red chilli, deseeded and thinly sliced into rounds, plus extra, to serve
220g cooked peeled 'cold water' prawns
6 radishes, trimmed and shaved with a vegetable peeler
50g roasted peanuts, roughly chopped
1 small bunch mint, leaves removed

For the egg noodles (makes 300g)
150g Tipo '00' flour or plain spelt
½ teaspoon salt
¼ teaspoon bicarbonate of soda
2 duck eggs
2 tablespoons cold water
tapioca flour or rice flour, for dusting

For the peanut dressing
2 tablespoons clear honey
3 tablespoons smooth peanut butter
1 lime, half juiced, half thinly sliced into half-moons
1 tablespoon toasted sesame oil
2 tablespoons light soy sauce

Make the egg noodles by mixing all the ingredients – except the tapioca flour – in a bowl and bringing together to make a ball. Rest for 10 minutes. Turn out onto a floured work surface and bang out the dough with a rolling pin; fold and rest for 20 minutes. Repeat four times. Cut into four and roll out a portion at a time as thinly as possible. Fold into four lengthways and slice into 0.5cm noodles, then separate out and toss in tapioca or rice flour to coat lightly and stop them sticking together. Or roll using a pasta machine – though I like to cut by hand even when I use the machine.

Half-fill a large pan with boiling water and bring it back to the boil. Cook the noodles for about 3 minutes until just *al dente*. Scoop out with a slotted spoon, refresh in cold water, then drain again. Keep the pan of boiling water ready over a low heat to reheat the noodles later.

To make the dressing, mix all the ingredients together in a bowl until smooth. Set aside.

Bring a pan of fresh water to the boil and lower the heat before gently adding the eggs (this prevents cracking the shell). Immediately increase the heat to a simmer and cook for 5 minutes, drain and refresh briefly in cold water before peeling. Add them to a bowl of hot water.

Meanwhile, drain the spring onions, rinse to get rid of the strong onion water and pat dry on kitchen paper. Heat a wok and add the oil, followed quickly by the fennel, and stir-fry for 2 minutes. Add the spring onions and chilli and stir-fry for a further minute before adding the prawns.

Reheat the noodles in the pan of boiling water, drain and toss with the dressing. Serve with the stir-fry in bowls and top with the sliced radishes, peanuts and mint. Lift the eggs onto kitchen paper, then place on top of each serving, adding the extra chilli.

Bubble & squeak with pork & crispy eggs

You can revert to sprouts at Christmas or spinach for this if you prefer, but I like spring greens at any time, and with the addition of pulled pork ham hock (now available ready prepared for you in packs at the supermarket), this is a wonderful dish for any meal. Even a can of corned beef would work instead of pork, so go retro and search some out to keep in the larder for emergencies.

enough for 4

650g King Edward or other floury
   potatoes for mashing, peeled
3 tablespoons rapeseed oil
1 garlic clove, crushed to a paste
   with a few sea salt crystals
about 50g spring greens, sliced
   lengthways, then shredded
90g pulled pork ham hock or
   cooked and shredded ham
freshly ground black pepper
5 medium eggs

Cut the potatoes into medium-sized pieces, add to a pan of boiling salted water and cook for about 15 minutes or until soft. Drain and mash.

Meanwhile, heat 1 tablespoon of the oil in a frying pan over a medium heat. Add the garlic and, as soon as it sizzles, add the spring greens and a splash of water. Cover and cook for about 4 minutes. Drain well and mix into the mash.

Mix in the pulled pork ham hock and season with pepper. Crack one of the eggs into a bowl, whisk with a fork and mix into the mash. Wipe out the frying pan and heat another tablespoon of the oil, add the mash mixture and fry for about 3 minutes. When it is golden on one side, break up the mixture and fry for a further 3 minutes until speckled golden brown.

Meanwhile, add the rest of the oil to a wok over a medium heat. Crack the remaining eggs into the oil one at a time and fry for about 3 minutes until crispy and frilly around the edges with the yolk done to your liking. Serve right away with the bubble and squeak.

hard-boiled

Devilled crab eggs

A bit of a retro recipe, but an egg book without a devilled egg would be sacrilege. If crab isn't your favourite thing, open a can of tuna steak and drain well before adding. Arrange the egg halves on a large platter and serve with a cocktail or two.

enough for 4

6 large eggs
2 teaspoons Dijon mustard
2 tablespoons mayonnaise (see page 14), or use shop-bought
½ teaspoon chilli powder
5g dill fronds, some chopped, some reserved for the top
100g pot of handpicked white crabmeat
1 teaspoon pul biber red pepper flakes
sea salt crystals

Bring a pan of water to the boil, then lower the heat before gently adding the eggs (this prevents cracking the shell). Immediately increase the heat to a simmer and cook for 8 minutes. Drain the eggs, refresh briefly in cold water, then crack and peel right away —even while still hot, as they are easier to peel. Put into cold water to cool completely.

Drain the eggs and gently pat them dry with kitchen paper. Cut each egg in half lengthways, flop out the yolks into a bowl and arrange the whites on a serving dish. Add the mustard, mayonnaise and chilli powder to the yolks and mash together with a pinch of salt.

Lightly fold in the chopped dill and crabmeat, then pile the mixture into the egg white halves. Sprinkle over some red pepper flakes and add a dill frond to the top of each just before serving.

hard-boiled

Leeks vinaigrette with eggs mimosa

Classically, very young, thin leeks are used whole for this dish, so do use if you find them, but you can still make this at any time of year – simply slice leeks diagonally and cook with butter and oil in a covered pan. This is rather good eaten with pickled herrings – easily found and inexpensive.

enough for 4 as a starter or more if sharing plates for a larger feast

400g (around 12) thin leeks, trimmed
3 medium eggs
1 teaspoon Dijon mustard
1 tablespoon white balsamic vinegar
3 tablespoons extra virgin olive oil
15 tiny whole black olives, stones in
10g flat-leaf parsley, leaves removed and chopped
2 tablespoons small capers, drained
sea salt crystals and freshly ground black pepper

Slit open the leeks from top to bottom, leaving the root end attached, and rinse under the cold tap to remove any grit. Add them to a pan of boiling salted water and cook for about 8 minutes until just tender. Drain and refresh in a basin of cold water.

Meanwhile, bring another pan of water to the boil, then lower the heat before gently adding the eggs – this prevents cracking the shells. Immediately increase the heat to a simmer and cook for 9 minutes. Drain the eggs and refresh briefly in cold water, then crack and peel right away – even when still hot as they are easier to peel. Put into the cold water with the leeks.

To make the dressing, put the mustard, vinegar, oil and seasoning in a jar with a tight lid and shake furiously to emulsify.

Drain the leeks and eggs and pat dry with kitchen paper. Halve the eggs across, pop out the yolks and grate them on a fine grater (to resemble mimosa blossoms). Chop the whites into small cubes.

Arrange the leeks on a serving dish and scatter over the olives, parsley, capers and chopped egg white. Spoon over the dressing and add the egg yolk mimosa to the top.

souffléd

Spezzatelle – a big bowl soufflé

This is inspired by a recipe from the Foggia region of Puglia in the southeast of Italy. I find dandelions aplenty in my garden at home, but you can forage young dandelion leaves before they flower from the countryside. That said, a few flowers taken from older plants make a pretty garnish to add to the finished dish. Pick them in places they're away from pathways and roads, and wash them well – it's easy, cheap and delicious – or you could use spinach.

enough for 4

100g young dandelion leaves,
    plus about 6 flower heads
75g butter, plus extra, for greasing
100g pancetta rashers
40g white spelt flour
450ml double cream
110g soft goat's cheese, without
    rind
75g Fontina or Gruyère cheese
50g Pecorino cheese, plus a little
    extra for topping
5 medium eggs
pinch of cream of tartar
sea salt crystals and freshly
    ground black pepper

Soak the dandelion leaves in lots of cold water for an hour or so. Preheat the oven to 230°C/gas mark 8. Wilt the dandelions for a few minutes in boiling salted water, drain and refresh under cold water, then drain again. Squeeze out all the excess water and chop finely. Grease a 30cm shallow ovenproof dish with butter and add the dandelions.

Cut the pancetta rashers into 1cm pieces with scissors (no need to separate as they separate themselves in the pan), add to a cold frying pan and stir-fry over a medium heat for a few minutes until they separate into golden wafers and the fat flows into the pan. Lift the pieces into the dandelions and wipe the fat from the pan.

Melt the butter, add the flour and cook for a minute. Stir in the cream and bring to a simmer until it thickens a little. Add the three cheeses, season and mix well. Pour into a large bowl and leave to cool for 5 minutes.

Separate the eggs, putting the whites into a large bowl with the cream of tartar and the yolks into a small one. Use hand-held electric beaters to whisk the whites until the beaters leave a pattern in the foam. Without washing the beaters, whisk the egg yolks into the cheese sauce. Gently fold in the egg whites, half at a time, and transfer to the greased dish. Scatter with a little extra Pecorino and bake in the oven for 10–15 minutes until puffed and golden. Serve at once, garnished with the danelion flowers.

scrambled

Green eggs & ham

It took a few attempts to get this mixture just right so I could show my esteem for the great Dr Seuss and his wonderful 'Green Eggs and Ham' story. It's simple to make the chlorophyll that maintains the strong green colour when heated. I leave you with his lovely quote: 'Today you are you! That is truer than true! There is no one alive who is you-er than you!'

enough for 6

100g spinach
20g flat-leaf parsley
10g basil
4 large eggs
150ml double cream
50ml full-fat milk
50g Gruyère cheese, finely grated
6 slices of your favourite bread
15g butter, plus extra for buttering
   the toast
about 300g ham, cut roughly from
   a small piece of shop-bought
   cooked ham or gammon
sea salt crystals and freshly
   ground black pepper
salad leaves and vinaigrette,
   to serve

Blend the spinach, parsley and basil with 200ml water until very smooth. Pour into a muslin-lined sieve set over a small pan to catch the liquid and squeeze gently to get all the green liquid out. Discard the fibre left behind, give the muslin a rinse and a squeeze and use to line the sieve again. Bring the pan of green liquid to a simmer for 1 minute until the chlorophyll separates on the surface and the water underneath becomes clear (keep checking for the clear liquid).

Pour into the muslin-lined sieve to catch the solids – this time keep the solids and discard the clear liquid. What you will be left with in the muslin is a green paste; scrape it off with a knife into a small bowl. Cover with clingfilm and set aside. Leave the muslin in the sieve and sit it over a bowl.

Crack the eggs into a bowl and add the chlorophyll paste, cream, milk and Gruyère, season and whisk. When the mixture is smooth there will be flecks, so if you want to maximise the green colour, pass the mixture through the muslin, pushing every last drop through using a ladle in a circular motion, or use the mixture as it comes with flecks in. This mixture sits happily, covered, in the fridge overnight.

Toast the bread how you like it and butter it. Melt the 15g of butter in a large-based pan or frying pan over a low–medium heat. When it starts to sizzle, pour in the egg mixture and stir with a wooden spoon, scraping the cooked egg into the runny mixture from around the edges as it sets. Continue to stir into curds for 2–3 minutes until the mixture is as you like a scramble to be.

Pile the scramble onto the toast, top with the roughly cut ham and serve with some dressed salad leaves.

baked

Ricotta, olive & asparagus terrine with herb oil

This makes a lovely posh supper dish served with some bright green herb oil and a scattering of nasturtium flowers and leaves or purple chive flower petals, when available. It's good with a salad of multi-coloured heritage tomatoes.

enough for 4–6

butter, for greasing
4 asparagus spears, trimmed
    and peeled
250g ricotta
4 medium eggs
1 medium egg yolk
2 tablespoons fine cornmeal
50g Parmesan cheese, finely grated
10 black olives, sliced off the
    stone lengthways
10 sun-dried tomatoes, drained
    and chopped
5g parsley or chervil
5g tarragon
5g chives
sea salt crystals and freshly
    ground black pepper

For the herb oil
5g parsley or chervil
5g tarragon
5g chives
100ml extra virgin olive oil

To serve
nasturtium leaves and flowers
4 heritage tomatoes of different
    colours, sliced

To make the herb oil, pull the parsley and tarragon leaves from the stalks, roughly chop along with the chives. Put in a mini processor with the oil and whizz to a paste. Pass the mixture through a fine sieve set over a bowl and leave to drip. Discard the solids and set the oil aside.

Preheat the oven to 180°C/gas mark 4. Grease a 0.75-litre loaf tin (even if nonstick) with butter and line the sides and base with baking paper.

Cut the asparagus in half lengthways and cook in boiling salted water for 2 minutes until just tender. Drain and refresh in cold water, drain again and dry on kitchen paper. Cut into 2cm lengths and set aside.

Put the ricotta in a bowl and whisk in the eggs and yolk, one at a time. Mix the cornmeal, grated Parmesan, a pinch of salt and some pepper together and whisk into the mixture. Stir in the olives and sun-dried tomatoes.

Pull the parsley and tarragon leaves from the stalks, chop along with the chives and fold into the mixture. Spoon a little into the loaf tin and add half the asparagus, then more ricotta mixture and the remaining asparagus, and finish with a layer of the ricotta mixture. Put into a roasting tin and add hot water to come half-way up the sides of the loaf tin. Bake in the oven for 35–45 minutes until risen, pale golden and set.

Remove the loaf tin from the water and sit it on a rack; as the terrine cools it will shrink a little. Leave to get cold before carefully transferring the terrine from the tin to a serving dish or board. Slice with a serrated (bread) knife and serve with the nasturtium leaves and flowers, tomatoes and the herb oil spooned over.

boiled

Quail egg coco-nutty curry with cashew nut sprinkles

A great dish for reheating as it's even tastier the day after. Serve with poppadoms and brown basmati rice, if you wish. Tiny bantam eggs work just as well if you can get them.

enough for 4

2 tablespoons raw coconut oil
350g onions, finely chopped
4 garlic cloves, crushed to a paste
    with a few sea salt crystals
1 lemongrass stem, finely sliced,
    then chopped
2cm piece of ginger, scraped
    and grated finely
1 tablespoon freshly ground
    coriander seeds
1 teaspoon freshly ground cumin
    seeds
1½ teaspoons turmeric powder
400g tomatoes, peeled, deseeded
    and finely chopped
juice of 1 lime
250ml coconut cream
400g can chickpeas, drained
    and rinsed
25g desiccated coconut
65g raw cashew nuts, lightly
    toasted
15g bunch coriander, leaves
    removed
12 quail eggs
sea salt crystals

To serve (optional)
cooked brown basmati rice
poppadoms
lime wedges

Heat the oil in a medium heavy-based pan and fry the onions, garlic, lemongrass and ginger for 10–15 minutes over a medium heat until pale golden. Add the spices, tomatoes and lime juice and cook for 3 minutes. Stir in the coconut cream and chickpeas, season to taste with salt and cook for a further 5 minutes.

Meanwhile, dry-roast the desiccated coconut in a frying pan for a few minutes, stirring all the time until golden, then tip onto a plate. Finely chop the cashews and most of the coriander, mix into the coconut and set aside.

Cook the quail eggs in boiling water for 2 minutes. Refresh briefly in cold water, crack the shells and peel right away (easier when just cooked) from the rounded end.

When ready to serve, gently fold the quail eggs into the hot curry and leave to heat for a few minutes. Serve in bowls with rice, poppadoms and lime wedges, if you wish, and sprinkle with the cashew nut mixture and the rest of the coriander leaves.

in the pan

Rice, spinach & eggs with feta

Quick, nutritious and delicious comfort food ready in around 30 minutes. The dill transforms the dish, so try not to leave it out unless you must! Put in as many eggs as people you are feeding.

enough for up to 4

100g basmati rice
175g young leaf spinach
5 tablespoons extra virgin olive oil
1 bunch spring onions, trimmed
    and chopped
2 garlic cloves, crushed to a paste
    with a few sea salt crystals
25g dill fronds
250ml water or vegetable stock
4 large eggs
100g feta cheese, sliced into shards
sea salt crystals and freshly
    ground black pepper

Soak the rice in cold water with a teaspoon of salt for 10 minutes.

Meanwhile, put the spinach in a large bowl and pour over boiling water. Leave for a minute, then drain and refresh in cold water, drain again and set aside.

Heat the oil in a shallow flameproof casserole about 21cm in diameter and fry the spring onions for a minute, stir in the garlic and turn off the heat.

Drain the rice, rinse and drain again and add to the spring onions. Use scissors to roughly snip the dill straight onto the rice, leaving any thick stalks behind to discard. Pour over the water or stock, season with salt and plenty of black pepper and bring quickly to a simmer. Turn the heat to low, cover and cook for 8 minutes.

Fold in the spinach, make four indentations in the mixture and crack in the eggs. Cover and cook for 8 minutes or until the egg whites are opaque and cooked and the yolks still soft. Serve with the feta scattered over.

steamed

My clean green glow bowl of goodness with ginger dressing

You can make this ahead and steam to heat up with an egg or two nestled in the middle or eat once cooked with a poached egg on top. Dress the leaves in the serving bowl with this ginger dressing as you come to eat and don't forget to add a few crunched-up nuts and seeds as well as the sliced avocado – a calming creamy addition to a Zen meal.

enough for 2

a few spoons of black beans from
   a carton or can, rinsed
4 stringless beans, shredded
6 tenderstem broccoli tips or
   florets from a head of broccoli
100g shelled edamame beans
50g shelled fresh or frozen peas
½ x 300g packet of tofu, cubed
½ x 250g packet ready-to-eat red
   and white quinoa
4 medium eggs
½ avocado, peeled, sliced and
   doused in the juice of 1 lime
lightly toasted hazelnuts, sunflower
   and sesame seeds, crunched up

For the ginger dressing
1½ tablespoons mirin
3 tablespoons fish sauce
juice of 1 lime
25g piece of ginger, scraped
2 teaspoons toasted sesame oil
4 tablespoons sunflower oil

To serve
coriander or other herb leaves
china rose sprouts or alfalfa

To make the dressing, put the mirin, fish sauce and lime juice in a screw-topped jar. Grate the ginger finely and squeeze the juice from the pulp into the jar, discarding the solids. Add the oils, screw on the lid and shake together to emulsify.

Toss the black beans in some of the dressing. Cook the shredded beans and broccoli in boiling salted water for 2 minutes. Add the edamame and peas for 30 seconds, drain, refresh in cold water and drain again.

Have a large pan with 3cm cold water in the bottom and a steaming rack or scrunched up foil in the bottom at the ready (or a traditional bamboo steamer set over the water). Arrange the cooked veg in a large heatproof bowl for one serving (keep the rest for another day or prepare another bowl for someone else to eat right away). Add some tofu, beans and quinoa, leaving a space for the eggs. Crack in two eggs per serving, put the bowl in the steamer, cover and heat for about 5 minutes until everything is hot and the eggs are cooked to your liking. Top with avocado, scatter with nuts, seeds, coriander and sprouts, spoon over some dressing and serve.

soufflèd

Roasted butternut & cheese soufflés

When adding whisked egg whites, always fold them in gently so as not to deflate the mixture and never whisk or stir after adding. Dusting the insides of the dishes with Parmesan after greasing gives the soufflé something to hang onto while doing its all-important high rise. For this recipe, I sometimes replace the butternut squash with sweet potato or pumpkin. It would also work as one large soufflé.

---

enough for 4 individual
or 6 smaller size

350g butternut squash (use the
    neck end)
2 teaspoons rapeseed oil
35g butter, plus extra for greasing
100g Parmesan cheese, finely
    grated, plus 2 tablespoons
    for dusting
40g plain flour
2 teaspoons Dijon mustard
150g full-fat milk
4 medium eggs
pinch of cream of tartar
sea salt crystals and freshly
    ground black pepper

Preheat the oven to 200°C/gas mark 6 and line a baking sheet with foil. Quarter the butternut lengthways and place on the lined baking sheet. Spoon over the oil, season and cook in the oven for about 40 minutes until soft.

Meanwhile, grease 4 x 250ml soufflé dishes with the extra butter and dust with the extra 2 tablespoons finely grated Parmesan.

Put the butter in a small pan and melt over a low heat. Whisk in the flour and mustard. Gradually pour in the milk, whisking continuously until smooth. Stir in the Parmesan and, when it melts, remove from the heat. Scoop the flesh from the cooked butternut skin, mash until very smooth and mix into the pan.

Separate the eggs, putting the yolks in a medium bowl and the whites in a separate one with the cream of tartar. Add the butternut mixture gradually to the egg yolks and mix well. Use hand-held electric beaters to whisk the whites until the beaters leave a pattern in the foam, then fold into the butternut mixture.

Spoon an equal quantity into each soufflé dish, about 0.5cm from the top, put on a baking tray and bake in the oven for about 20 minutes until puffed and golden. Serve right away.

baked

Mushroom eggs en cocotte

Baked eggs can be made for one or for as many guests as you have to serve, even at the drop of a hat! You could follow the other flavour options below, keeping the method the same.

enough for 4

butter, for greasing
2 teaspoons rapeseed oil
150g small chestnut mushrooms, sliced
1 garlic clove, crushed to a paste with a few sea salt crystals
120ml crème fraîche
20g Parmesan cheese, finely grated
4 small eggs or 8 quail eggs
a few chives, chopped
sea salt crystals and freshly ground black pepper
wafer-thin toast, to serve

Preheat the oven to 200°C/gas mark 6. Grease 4 x 150ml ramekins or small bowls with butter. Heat the rapeseed oil in a frying pan over a medium heat, add the mushrooms and stir-fry until no moisture remains and they are cooked through. Add the garlic and stir for another minute.

Season the crème fraiche and divide half of it between the ramekins, then add equal quantities of the mushrooms and a scattering of Parmesan. Crack an egg into each. Spoon more crème fraiche onto the tops, avoiding the yolks, and add a tiny touch of Parmesan. Put into a roasting tin and pour in some hot water to come half-way up the sides of the ramekins. Cover with dampened, squeezed-out baking paper and bake in the oven for 12–15 minutes or until the whites are cooked and the yolks still runny or cooked to your liking. Add some chives and serve with toast for dunking.

More Ideas

Smoked salmon – Divide 100g smoked salmon between the ramekins and add chopped dill. Leave out the Parmesan.

Brown shrimp – Divide a 90g packet of peeled brown shrimps between the ramekins and add chopped flat-leaf parsley. Leave out the Parmesan.

Feta – Crumble 100g feta between the ramekins, add lots of mixed fresh herbs, such as parsley, oregano and basil and leave out the Parmesan.

fried

Eggs with aubergine, onions, parsley, feta & pine nuts

I like simplicity in a dish and adding different ingredients can change it easily, so use what you have to hand. You could add spices or just chilli, or mozzarella instead of feta so it melts a little in the pan, leeks perhaps instead of onion. Either coriander or parsley work. Cook this all together in one big pan or in individual smaller pans, if that's what you have.

enough for 2

2 thin aubergines
4 tablespoons rapeseed oil
1 large onion, halved top to
   bottom and finely sliced across
2 garlic cloves, crushed to a paste
   with a few sea salt crystals
10g flat-leaf parsley, leaves taken
   off the stems
4 medium eggs
1 tablespoon toasted pine nuts
25g feta cheese, crumbled
sea salt crystals and freshly
   ground black pepper

Preheat the grill to high and set the shelf about 15cm from the heat. Slice the aubergine into 5mm slices and put on a baking tray. Spoon over 2 tablespoons of the oil and toss to roughly coat the slices. Grill for 4–5 minutes on each side or until cooked and golden.

Meanwhile, heat the rest of the oil in a frying pan with a base about 20cm across and fry the onion over a low–medium heat for about 9 minutes until soft and golden. Add the garlic and stir-fry for a minute before gently mixing in the aubergine slices (they shouldn't break down) with the parsley leaves. Season well, then crack the eggs into the spaces and fry until the whites are cooked and the yolks still soft.

Scatter over the pine nuts, crumbled feta and a grinding of pepper. Serve with a few sea salt crystals to season the eggs.

A bowl of chicken & egg comfort

This bowl of goodness is based on the Greek avgolemono. Of course the Ancient Greeks were very much into egg cookery from around 500BC, but the egg and lemon combination most probably originated much later. I don't usually like to use vinegar in egg poaching but in this instance it's fine as the eggs go into a lemony-flavoured stock.

enough for 4

1 tablespoon extra virgin olive oil
1 onion, finely chopped
2 garlic cloves, crushed to a paste
    with a few sea salt crystals
4 skinless chicken thigh fillets or
    2 breasts
500ml good homemade or
    shop-bought chicken stock
6 medium eggs
splash of wine vinegar
2 unwaxed lemons
150g orzo pasta
sea salt crystals and freshly ground
    black pepper
50g freshly grated Parmesan
    cheese, to serve
20g flat-leaf parsley, leaves
    removed, to serve

Heat the oil over a medium heat and fry the onion for 4 minutes to soften. Add the garlic, chicken thighs, stock and 500ml water. Bring to a gentle simmer and cook for 15–20 minutes until the chicken is just tender.

Meanwhile, poach four of the eggs, one at a time. Have a pan of boiling water ready and add a tiny splash of wine vinegar. Swirl the water and crack the first egg into the vortex, turn off the heat and time for 2½ minutes. When the egg is ready, lift into a bowl of cold water and continue poaching the other three eggs in the same way.

Finely zest one of the lemons and set the zest aside in a small bowl. Thinly pare off the rind from the other, shred it finely, put in another small bowl and cover for serving later. Juice both the lemons into a medium bowl, crack in the remaining two eggs and whisk with a fork, then set aside.

When the chicken is ready, lift it out of the stock and put onto a plate. Continue to simmer the stock gently. Add the orzo and fine lemon zest to the stock with a pinch of salt and cook for 8 minutes or until the orzo is almost cooked. Shred or slice the chicken thinly and return to the stock.

Fill a bowl or pan with boiling water and gently lift the poached eggs into the water to heat through for a minute. Gradually mix a few ladlefuls of the hot stock into the lemon and egg mixture, then add this mixture to the pan of hot stock and turn off the heat. Stir well and serve in large bowls each topped with a hot poached egg, shredded lemon rind, Parmesan and parsley leaves. Season to taste.

boiled

Potato, avocado, quail eggs & bacon with crispy shallots

I love potatoes and eggs together in a salad, letting the warm potatoes drink up the dressing, and, with crispy lardons and shallots, what's not to like?

enough for 4

100ml extra virgin olive oil
4 banana shallots, finely sliced
12 quail eggs
1 tablespoon white balsamic
   vinegar
500g new potatoes
75g smoked bacon lardons
1 large avocado
sea salt crystals and freshly
   ground black pepper
rocket leaves and flowers, to serve

Heat a large wok over a medium heat, add the 90ml oil and the shallots, then lower the heat a little and stir regularly so the shallots turn an even golden colour without burning. Place a metal sieve over a bowl and have a plate lined with kitchen paper at the ready. When the shallots are golden, pour them and the oil into the sieve, then tip onto the lined plate and spread out to cool and crisp up.

Bring a pan of water to the boil and lower the heat before gently adding the eggs – this prevents cracking the shells. Immediately increase the heat to a simmer and cook for 2½ minutes. Drain the eggs, put into cold water, then crack and peel right away from the rounded end (they are easier to peel while still slightly hot). Pop into cold water and set aside.

To prepare the dressing, put the vinegar in a small bowl, season with ground black pepper and sea salt crystals and whisk in the remaining extra virgin olive oil.

Put the potatoes in a medium pan of boiling salted water and simmer for 20 minutes or until just tender. Drain, slice into rounds and put on a serving platter. While they are still hot, pour over the dressing and toss together.

Put a frying pan on a high heat, add the bacon lardons and stir-fry until golden and crisp. Lift out onto the potatoes (leaving the fat behind to discard when cold) and mix. Cut the avocado in half, remove the stone, peel, slice and arrange the pieces on top of the serving platter.

Cut the eggs in half and arrange over the top and add some ground black pepper. Scatter with the crispy shallots and the rocket leaves and flowers.

buttered in the pan

Puy lentils, spinach, anchovies & pine nuts with buttered duck eggs

If tackling two eggs at once bothers you, try one egg at a time until you perfect the technique for buttered eggs. Also, having someone on hand to keep the glass topped up with cracked eggs helps, that way you can keep the pan tilted with your spare hand so the eggs retain their compact shape. Otherwise, have all four eggs at the ready, cracked into separate glasses.

enough for 4

2 tablespoons rapeseed oil
6 anchovies in olive oil
2 garlic cloves, crushed to a paste
  with a few sea salt crystals
250g packet of ready-to-eat
  cooked Puy lentils
4 tablespoons toasted pine nuts
160g baby spinach
4 duck eggs
40g butter
freshly ground black pepper
mustard and cress, to serve

Put the oil, anchovies and garlic in a frying pan with a lid and warm them together over a low heat. Turn off the heat as soon as the garlic sizzles, which is only a matter of seconds, then stir to dissolve the anchovies. Tip the lentils into a colander and rinse under cold water to break them up, drain and add to the pan.

Put the spinach in a bowl and pour over boiling water, leave for a minute until wilted, drain well and add to the lentil mixture along with the pine nuts and pepper. Cover and put over a low heat to heat the lentils for a few minutes, no longer.

Crack one egg at a time into a small glass. Melt the butter in a saucepan and tilt it so the butter puddles, add the egg and spoon it onto itself to stop it spreading. When it firms up after a few seconds, add another egg and keep doing this with the pan tilted. Cook the other two in the same way. Baste with a spoon as they cook to golden underneath and look a little like a poached egg on the top. Serve on the lentil mixture with the butter from the pan spooned over, garnished with mustard and cress.

Sweet things
&
indulgences

baked custard

Passion fruit custard & jelly

Such alchemy takes place when passion fruit juice and heat get together. A jelly happens almost within seconds, making the perfect quick tangy topping for these passion fruit custards. Or you could scatter the tops with sugar and blowtorch to a crisp brulée and serve the jelly in a small bowl alongside. Keep the spare egg whites in a jar in the fridge for a week or in a tub in the freezer (see page 5).

enough for 6

9 passion fruit
300ml double cream
4 medium egg yolks
70g caster sugar

Cut the passion fruit in half and scoop the flesh out with a teaspoon straight into a blender. Whizz just to loosen the juice from the jelly-like seeds (you don't want to break up the black seeds). Push the resulting juice through a fine sieve into a small bowl, discarding the seeds that are left. Alternatively, put the flesh in a fine sieve set over a bowl and use the back of a ladle in a circular motion to push all the juice through, breaking up the jelly from around the seeds.

Preheat the oven to 180°C/gas mark 4 and place the shelf in the middle.

Pour the double cream into a small pan and heat until a few bubbles appear around the edge, then remove from the heat. Meanwhile, put the egg yolks and 65g of the sugar into a medium bowl and whisk with a balloon whisk until the sugar dissolves. Stir in 6 tablespoons of the passion fruit juice followed by the hot cream.

Set 6 x 100ml ramekins in a deep roasting tin and pour in the mixture evenly. Fill the tin with hot (not boiling) water to come half-way up the sides of the ramekins and scrunch up a piece of dampened and squeezed-out baking paper large enough to cover the whole tin. Bake in the oven for 25 minutes until the custards are just set with a slight wobble when moved. Leave for about 5 minutes, then carefully remove them from the water and leave to cool completely.

Put the rest of the passion fruit juice in a small pan with the remaining sugar. Heat gently and stir for about a minute or until the juice thickens to a jelly-like mixture. Cool for a few minutes, then pour a little over the surface of each custard, swirling gently so the mixture spreads to the edges. Put in the fridge until ready to serve.

cake

Mandarin & chocolate sformato

I simply love this Italian fatless and flourless cake with added sliced dark chocolate forming layers in the mixture, but it's okay to leave it out if you wish. Try to find firm, sweet mandarins of a pipless variety – though you could use any small firm oranges – provided you follow the weight given and still cook them whole.

enough for 8–10

350–400g (4 or 5) mandarins or
   small oranges
butter, for greasing
275g ground almonds
1 teaspoon natural orange extract
45g very dark chocolate (90 per
   cent or 85 per cent cocoa solids)
   plus an extra 35g, to decorate
4 medium eggs
125g golden caster sugar

Put the whole mandarins in a pan large enough to accommodate them in a single layer, pour in enough cold water just to cover them, then top with a circle of baking paper. Sit a plate over the oranges to stop them floating. Bring to the boil, half-cover with a lid and lower the heat to simmer for 10–15 minutes (longer if using oranges) until just tender. Drain well.

Preheat the oven to 160°C–180°C/gas mark 3–4. Grease the base and sides of a 19cm loose-bottomed square tin and line with baking paper.

Cut the mandarins into pieces (removing any pips) and put in a processor. Add the almonds and orange extract and whizz to a purée. Slice the chocolate into shards with a sharp knife and set aside.

Crack the eggs into a large bowl and whisk in the sugar until bubbly. Stir in the orange mixture a little at a time, mixing with a wooden spoon. Spoon about a third of the mixture into the tin and scatter with half the chocolate shards. Spoon in another third of the mixture and scatter with the remaining shards, then top with the rest of the mixture. Bake in the oven for 40 minutes, cover with tented foil and cook for 10–15 minutes until it feels firm to the touch. Remove from the oven and cool in the tin for 30 minutes. Unmould and place on a wire rack to cool completely.

To decorate, either slice the extra chocolate and scatter over the top of the cake or follow the next easy step to make professional-looking shards. Break the extra chocolate into a heatproof bowl large enough to sit over a pan of barely simmering water so the base of the bowl doesn't touch the water. Melt for 4 minutes, remove the bowl and stir until completely melted. Wet a small sheet of baking parchment then scrunch it up, open it out and lay it on a shelf in a hot oven and when it dries out (only a few minutes) lay it flat on a tray and smooth the chocolate over with a spatula.

Put the tray in the fridge and, when the chocolate is hard, carefully peel it off the paper and snap it into shards and decorate the top of the sformato (it gives a crinkled effect).

cake & meringue

Mocha meringue-topped brownies

This recipe uses 'cooked' Italian meringue, made with a hot sugar syrup, which is a little more stable than simple meringue. Minus its topping, the brownie is perfect for day-to-day eating as it keeps in an airtight container layered between sheets of baking paper for about a week. Once it is topped with meringue, eat within a couple of days.

enough for 9 or more squares

125g butter, roughly cubed and
    left at room temperature, plus
    extra for greasing
250g dark chocolate (70 per cent
    cocoa solids)
125g organic coconut sugar
100g ground almonds
1 tablespoon instant espresso
    powder
2 tablespoons cocoa powder
6 medium eggs

For the meringue topping
165g caster sugar
3 medium egg whites
pinch of cream of tartar
1 teaspoon instant espresso
    powder

Preheat the oven to 180°C/gas mark 4. Grease the base and sides of a 19cm square loose-bottomed tin with sides 6cm deep and line with baking paper.

Break the chocolate into squares and put in a heatproof bowl and sit over a pan of barely simmering water, not letting the base of the bowl touch the water. Melt for 5 minutes, remove the bowl, stir until smooth and set aside.

Put the butter and all but 2 tablespoons of the sugar in a large bowl and whisk together until soft and fluffy. Sift the ground almonds, espresso powder and cocoa powder into another bowl and set aside. Crack four of the eggs into a small bowl and separate the other two, adding the yolks to the whole eggs and the whites to another bowl.

Whisk the whites until the beaters leave a pattern in the foam and add the remaining 2 tablespoons of sugar a little at a time, whisking well between each addition. Without washing the beaters, whisk the whole eggs and yolks a little at a time into the butter and sugar mixture until smooth. Beat in the chocolate with a wooden spoon, then add the almond mixture a little at a time until smooth. Fold in the stiff egg whites.

Pour into the prepared tin and bake in the oven for 30–35 minutes. The cake will be starting to crack slightly around the edges. Put the tin on a wire rack and leave for 10 minutes. Remove the cake from the tin, leaving the paper in place, and leave to cool completely. Firm it up in the fridge overnight or put in a cold place.

Up to a few hours before serving, cut into as many pieces as you like and arrange on a baking sheet ready for the topping. Put 5 tablespoons just-boiled water in a medium pan, add the caster sugar, stir and set aside for 5 minutes. Put over a low heat to dissolve the sugar completely and, when the mixture is clear, increase the heat and bring to the boil.

If you have a thermometer, place in the syrup and when it reaches 115°C it's ready to use. Alternatively boil the syrup for 2½ minutes, keeping a close eye on it so it doesn't caramelise. Meanwhile, using hand-held electric beaters, whisk the egg whites with the cream of tartar until the beaters leave a pattern in the foam.

When the sugar syrup is ready, gradually pour it into the whites, whisking continuously (avoid pouring the hot syrup onto the beaters) until stiff. Place the bowl in a bigger basin of cold water so it comes half-way up the sides and continue to whisk for 4 minutes until cold. Sprinkle with the espresso powder and gently fold it into the meringue.

Spoon the meringue into a piping bag fitted with a 1cm plain nozzle and pipe over the brownie. Alternatively, just spoon it over and swirl the top.

Preheat the grill to high and put the shelf in the middle. Put the decorated brownie squares under the hot grill for about 45 seconds (watch very carefully) until the meringue is pale golden in parts. Use a palette knife to transfer to a serving plate.

baked

Blueberry & white chocolate cheesecake

I love a baked cheesecake and this luscious dessert is one everyone gets excited about. I always have some crunchy amaretti tucked away in a tin left from Christmas, and they inspired this recipe as blueberries marry so well with amaretti. Make this a day ahead so it sets firm in the fridge.

enough for 8–10

butter, for greasing
4 large eggs
200g crunchy amaretti
2 tablespoons plain flour
350g Belgian white chocolate
250ml double cream
300g mascarpone
75g caster sugar
300g blueberries
sifted icing sugar, for dusting

Grease a deep-sided 24cm round springform tin and line with baking paper. Preheat the oven to 170°C/gas mark 3 and put a baking sheet on the middle shelf to heat up.

Crack three of the eggs into a bowl and separate the fourth egg, putting the white in a small bowl and adding the yolk to the other whole eggs. Put the amaretti and flour into a processor and whizz to a fine crumb. Add the egg white and whizz again to mix, then tip into the tin, pressing it evenly over the base. Chill in the fridge.

Break the chocolate into squares and put in a medium pan with the cream. Heat gently to melt the chocolate, stirring every few minutes so it doesn't stick to the base of the pan. When the chocolate has melted completely, cool the quick way by putting the base of the pan in a larger basin of cold water.

Whisk the mascarpone and sugar together and add the eggs one at a time, whisking until smooth, then stir in the cooled chocolate mixture. Pour one third of the mixture over the amaretti base and scatter over 100g of the blueberries. Pour over another third of the mixture, scatter with another 100g of blueberries and pour over the rest of the mixture.

Put the tin on the baking sheet and bake in the oven for about 1 hour 10 minutes – it should still have a slight wobble but the top will be tinged pale golden. Turn off the heat and leave in the oven for 30 minutes. Put the tin on a wire rack to cool for 1 hour. Gently remove the sides of the tin and put the cheesecake in the fridge overnight. To serve, scatter over the rest of the blueberries and sift over a little icing sugar.

custard & batter

Creamy elderflower dipping custard with elderflower tempura

Forage the freshest elderflowers from unpolluted areas on a dry sunny day when the hedgerows are in bloom. Simply shake the heads to remove any insects.

Iris, who prop-styled this book, puts broken-up blossoms into crêpes. So give that a try, using the recipe for buckwheat crêpes on page 26, adding a little sugar to the batter as you whisk. If you can't find the flowers for the tempura, simply use this lovely custard with some cooked early-summer gooseberries – the flavours are magical together – or spoon it over fresh strawberries and raspberries.

enough for 6

For the dipping custard
175ml elderflower cordial
3 large eggs
3 tablespoons caster sugar
3 tablespoons extra thick
    double cream

For the tempura
about 18 elderflower heads
2 tablespoons caster sugar, plus
    about 1 tablespoon for dusting
sunflower oil, for deep-frying
1 large egg
250ml sparkling water
125g cornflour
125g fine rice flour
1 teaspoon bicarbonate of soda
1 teaspoon baking powder
pinch of sea salt crystals
1 large egg white

To make the dipping custard, heat the cordial in a pan and bring to a simmer. Crack the eggs into a bowl and whisk with the sugar, then pour the hot cordial into the mixture, whisking continuously. Pour this mixture back into the pan and stir over a low heat for about 10 minutes until thickened. If you have a thermometer, don't let the mixture reach over 75°C. Pour through a sieve set over a bowl, stir in the double cream and set aside to cool completely.

To make the tempura, the batter should be used as soon as it's made. Remove any tough stems from the elderflowers and set aside, keeping them dry. Line a tray with kitchen paper and have some caster sugar ready to sift over the top.

Heat the oil to 190°C in a deep heavy-based pan. Crack the whole egg into a large bowl and whisk in the sparkling water. Sift all the dry ingredients together, using 1 tablespoon of the sugar, and add to the liquid all in one go. Stir to mix – it doesn't need to be smooth. Whisk the egg white to a foam and whisk in the remaining tablespoon of sugar, then fold into the batter. Dip the flower heads into the batter and deep-fry in the hot oil a few at a time until crisp but not browned (lower the heat if it gets too hot). Drain on the lined tray and dust with the extra sugar. Serve at once with the dipping custard.

choux pastry,
custard & meringue

Rose meringeroles

These dainty mouthfuls of heaven are a coming-together of
my favourites, profiteroles and meringues. The choux balls are
filled with pastry cream, then either dipped into stiff meringue
or piped Turkish-turban-style, then blowtorched. The flavour of
rose isn't to everyone's taste so leave it out if you prefer. You can
fill and top them a few hours before serving, but they also keep
in the fridge for a few days – just bring to room temperature
before eating.

makes 20

For the pastry cream
300ml double cream
4 tablespoons full-fat milk
15g plain flour
15g cornflour
65g caster sugar
1 medium egg yolk
2 medium eggs
1 teaspoon rose water (optional)

For the choux pastry
65g butter, cubed
110g plain flour
3 medium eggs

For the meringue topping
2 medium egg whites
2 tablespoons just-boiled water
120g caster sugar
1 tablespoon liquid glucose
1½ teaspoons rose water (optional)

To make the pastry cream, put the cream and milk in a medium pan and
heat gently until bubbles start to appear around the edges. Put the flours
and sugar in a bowl and mix in the egg yolk to make a paste. Crack in the
whole eggs and whisk, slowly adding the hot cream.

Rinse the pan out, pour in the mixture and heat gently, stirring continuously
with a wooden spoon until it is thick and smooth (use a balloon whisk if
you need to). Pour into a clean bowl and stir in the rose water (if using),
cover the surface with clingfilm and leave to cool completely (for speed put
the bowl in a bigger basin of cold water), then chill until needed.

To make the choux pastry, preheat the oven to 200°C/gas 6 and have ready
two baking sheets (there is no need to grease or flour them). Put 200ml
cold water in a medium pan with the butter. Sift the flour onto a sheet
of baking paper. Heat the water over a medium heat until the butter has
melted and the water is just starting to fizz. Remove from the heat, shoot
in the flour all in one go and beat like mad with a wooden spoon until very
smooth. Cool for 5 minutes in the pan.

Crack the eggs into a bowl and break them up with a fork. Beat into the
mixture in the pan, a little at a time, until the mixture becomes firm and
glossy and holds its shape. Spoon 20 mounds (each about a heaped
teaspoonful) onto the baking sheets (or pipe using a plain 2cm nozzle).
Bake in the oven for 25–30 minutes until puffed and golden. Make a small
slit in the side of each one and put back into the oven to dry for a few
minutes. Put the choux balls on a wire rack to cool completely, then store
in an airtight container for up to two days or until ready to use.

Use a serrated knife to cut the choux balls half-way through horizontally.
Fill with the pastry cream and arrange again on the baking sheets.
For the meringue topping, put the egg whites into a large bowl and have

hand-held electric beaters at the ready. Put the water, sugar, glucose and rose water (if using) in a small pan and set over a low heat. When the sugar dissolves to a clear syrup, turn up the heat to medium and boil for 4 minutes or until the temperature reaches 115°C on a sugar thermometer. Immediately remove from the heat and put aside so the bubbles subside (if it is too hot, the whites overcook). Now start whisking the egg whites until the beaters leave patterns in the foam.

With the motor running, gradually pour in the hot syrup (avoiding the beaters!) and whisk until the meringue is stiff, glossy and cooled down. Pipe the meringue onto the profiteroles using a piping bag fitted with a 1cm star nozzle or dip them into the meringue (you may need to gently stir the meringue a little if you do it this way), lifting upwards so they have a cheeky point on top. Blowtorch the tops very briefly to tan lightly. Keep for up to 2 hours in a cool place before serving and keep any left over in the fridge for a few days.

Tiramisu with nut
& chocolate sprinkles

For me the important thing is a good strong coffee flavour in a tiramisu – so often this classic Italian dessert is a big let-down as frequently lacking in its namesake ingredient to 'pick me up'.

enough for 8

80g walnuts
100g dark chocolate (70% cocoa solids)
250ml strong espresso, cooled
100ml coffee liqueur
4 tablespoons calvados
4 medium eggs
85g caster sugar
250g mascarpone
200–250g sponge fingers (boudoir biscuits)

Roughly chop the walnuts and chocolate and whizz in a mini processor to a crumb. Mix the espresso, coffee liqueur and calvados together in a bowl.

Crack the eggs one at a time and separate the whites and yolks into different bowls (see page 5 for how to avoid getting any yolk into the whites). Whisk the whites until the beaters leave patterns in the foam, then add half the sugar a little at a time, whisking between each addition. Without washing the beaters, whisk the yolks and the rest of the sugar until pale and thick, then whisk in the mascarpone a little at a time until smooth. Fold the stiff whites into the mixture.

Have eight serving glasses lined up and start by dipping two sponge fingers at a time into the coffee mixture and arranging them in a glass, cutting them to fit. Make sure you don't over-soak the sponge fingers so they break into a mush – they still need a little crunch. Continue to arrange dipped sponge fingers in the other seven glasses.

Divide a third of the mascarpone mixture between the glasses and do the same with the nut and chocolate sprinkles. Continue layering the rest of the dipped sponge fingers, mascarpone and sprinkles in the same way, finishing with the sprinkles on the top. Chill overnight to set. They keep for a few days if kept chilled.

pastry & meringue

Raspberry meringue flan

This is even better if you can pick your own raspberries as they are firm and very tasty. You could just as easily use blackberries instead. Serve with pouring cream for extra indulgence.

enough for 8

50g lightly toasted hazelnuts, crushed

For the sweet flan pastry
190g plain flour
100g butter, softened
40g caster sugar
3 medium egg yolks

For the meringue
3 medium egg whites
pinch of cream of tartar
155g caster sugar
400g raspberries and a few redcurrants, when available
icing sugar, for dusting

To make the pastry, put all the ingredients in a processor and pulse until evenly coloured and just coming together. Depending on the temperature, you may find it too soft to roll right away; if so, flatten a little, wrap in clingfilm and chill for 15 minutes before rolling.

If the pastry is not too soft, roll out as soon as it is made on a sheet of baking paper and line a 24cm fluted loose-bottomed flan tin, using the paper to help position it in the tin. Press the pastry into the flutes and roll over the top with a rolling pin to trim off the excess, then chill for around 20 minutes.

Preheat the oven to 200°C/gas mark 6. Line the pastry with a sheet of scrunched-up baking paper, add baking beans and bake in the oven for 15 minutes. Remove the paper and beans and return to the oven for a further 8 minutes, then remove and set aside to cool.

Reduce the oven temperature to 110°C/gas mark ¼. Scatter the hazelnuts over the cooled flan case.

To make the meringue, put the egg whites and cream of tartar in a large bowl and whisk until firm and the beaters leave a pattern in the foam. Gradually add the sugar, whisking constantly until stiff and glossy.

Measure out 120g of the meringue and put in a small bowl. Add 300g of the raspberries to the remaining meringue and gently fold together. Spoon this mixture into the flan case and smooth down. Add the plain meringue to the top and smooth over with a palette knife. Dust with icing sugar and bake in the oven for 30 minutes until crisp. Serve warm with the rest of the raspberries arranged on the top with a few redcurrants if you have them and dusted with more icing sugar.

meringue

Plum meringue baked in a tray

This is just as nice without the pistachios and dried plum powder, but it is worth finding these ingredients in wholefood shops and Middle Eastern stores or online. You can use all golden caster sugar or half the quantity whizzed up with organic coconut sugar – you won't get a white meringue but a gorgeous buff one instead.

enough for 6

600g red plums, halved and
    stoned (quartered if large)
1 tablespoon caster sugar

For the meringue
4 large egg whites
¼ teaspoon cream of tartar
210g caster sugar
5 tablespoons pistachio nibs
    or skinned pistachios, roughly
    crushed (optional)
2 teaspoons dried plum powder
    (optional)

Put the plums in a pan with the sugar and 1 tablespoon water. Stir, cover and poach over a low heat for about 10 minutes until soft. Keep checking and stirring so they don't stick. Tip into an oven tray or ovenproof dish about 20 x 24cm with sides a few centimetres deep. Leave to cool.

Preheat the oven to 110°C/gas mark ¼.

To make the meringue, put the egg whites and cream of tartar in a large bowl. Use hand-held electric beaters to whisk until firm and the beaters leave a pattern in the foam. Gradually add the sugar, whisking constantly until stiff and glossy.

Fold through half the pistachios (if using). Spoon blobs of the meringue over the plums, making peaks as you lift the spoon away, then scatter with the rest of the nuts and dust with the plum powder. Bake in the oven for 35 minutes until the meringues are set firm. Serve hot or cold.

meringue

Apple & salted caramel petit Mont Blanc

This French classic usually involves chestnut purée, but I have used apple purée instead to give a sharpness that offsets the slightly bitter-sweet caramel. I like to eat these after they have sat in a cool place for a few hours as they turn deliciously gooey.

enough for 6

4 eating apples of good flavour
   and not too sweet
3 medium egg whites
pinch of cream of tartar
150g caster sugar
300ml double cream

For the caramel
100g caster sugar
¼ teaspoon sea salt crystals
   (optional)

Peel and slice the apples straight into a pan, add 2 tablespoons water, cover and cook over a medium heat for about 8 minutes, checking occasionally to make sure they don't burn. When they are soft, set aside to cool, then purée in a blender.

Preheat the oven to 110°C/gas mark ¼. Line two baking sheets with baking paper.

Put the egg whites and cream of tartar in a large bowl. Using hand-held electric beaters, whisk until firm and the beaters leave a pattern in the foam. Gradually add the sugar, whisking constantly until stiff and glossy. Dab a little of the meringue left on the beaters onto the four corners of each baking sheet to secure the baking paper in place.

Using about a third of the mixture, spoon 6 x 5–6cm blobs of meringue onto one of the baking sheets, creating a peak on top as you lift the spoon away. Using the rest of the mixture, spoon 6 x 7–8cm circles of meringue onto the other baking sheet for the bases and form a slight dip in the middle, using the back of the spoon to contain the apple and cream. Bake both trays in the oven for about 1 hour until the meringues lift off the paper easily. Cool completely on a wire rack.

Put the cream in a bowl, ready for the caramel. To make the caramel, put the sugar in a small pan with 4 tablespoons just-boiled water and stir to dissolve. Over a medium–high heat, boil the mixture to a rich amber colour. Remove from the heat and add 5 tablespoons of the cream. When the bubbles settle, add a tablespoon of this creamy caramel to the remaining cream in the bowl and whip to soft floppy peaks.

Divide the apple purée and the whipped mixture between the meringue bases. Top each one with a smaller meringue. If using salt, mix the salt into the creamy caramel and spoon over.

meringue

Marmalade pavlova roulade

This is so easy to put together and perfect for a little bit of indulgence. It isn't all that sweet, thanks to the tang of the marmalade, so take the trouble to find a really good one.

enough for 8–10

butter, for greasing
4 medium egg whites
pinch of cream of tartar
190g caster sugar
2 teaspoons cornflour
1 tablespoon icing sugar, plus
   extra for dusting
1 teaspoon white balsamic
   vinegar or white wine vinegar
finely grated zest of 2 large
   oranges
60g skinless hazelnuts, lightly
   roasted and finely chopped
300ml double cream
¼ teaspoon pure orange extract
   (optional)
4 tablespoons medium-cut
   marmalade, or fine if preferred

Preheat the oven to 160°C/gas mark 3. Grease a 25 x 34cm baking tray with sides 4cm deep with a sheet of baking paper large enough to come up the sides.

Put the egg whites and cream of tartar in a large bowl. Use hand-held electric beaters to whisk until firm and the beaters leave a pattern in the foam. Gradually add the sugar, whisking constantly until stiff and glossy.

Sift the cornflour and icing sugar over the meringue and gently fold in using a large metal spoon. Add the vinegar and gently fold through so as not to lose volume. Spoon the meringue into the prepared baking tray (don't worry if it looks like there isn't enough mixture; there is!), level off with a spatula and bake in the oven for 20 minutes.

Line a wire rack with baking paper and sift over a liberal amount of icing sugar. Cool the pavlova for a few minutes, then tip out onto the icing sugar. Remove the lining paper and leave to cool completely.

Mix the orange zest and finely chopped nuts together and scatter about half over the pavlova. Whip the cream in a bowl with the orange extract until soft peaks form. Fold the marmalade into the cream, a spoonful at a time, and spread it evenly over the surface of the pavlova to within a centimetre of the edges, taking care not to dislodge the zest and nut mixture. Shallowly score one of the short edges of the pavlova and start to fold into a roulade with the help of the baking paper. Lift onto a serving dish, scatter the rest of the zest and nut mixture down the middle of the roulade and sift over more icing sugar. Chill until ready to serve, then cut into thick slices.

Tangy lemon tartlets

Classic sharp lemon tartlets make the perfect dessert or a treat for tea. The crisp tart shells will keep, still in the tins, stored in an airtight container, for a few days. If you have done this, when you come to bake the filling you need to heat the pastry for a few minutes first. Dust with icing sugar and serve with softly whipped double cream or pouring cream if you like.

makes 8 individual tarts

90g butter, at room temperature
65g caster sugar
3 medium egg yolks
210g plain flour
65g ground almonds
1 medium egg white, for glazing
    the pastry

For the filling
6 medium eggs
200g caster sugar
6 lemons, 1 finely zested and all
    of them juiced (you need 200ml
    of juice)
300ml double cream

Use a wooden spoon to beat the butter and sugar together until well mixed and soft. Beat in the egg yolks one at a time, beating until the sugar is no longer gritty and the mixture is stiff. Mix in the flour and almonds. Tip onto a sheet of clingfilm and bring the mixture into a ball, flatten a little and wrap the clingfilm around it. Chill for 30 minutes–1 hour until just firm.

Divide the dough into eight pieces and thinly roll out one piece at a time between sheets of baking paper. Use to line eight loose-bottomed 10cm x 3cm deep fluted tart tins. Press the pastry into the flutes and roll over the top with a rolling pin to trim the excess pastry. Prick the pastry bases with a fork and chill for 20 minutes or overnight.

Preheat the oven to 200°C/gas mark 6. Put a baking sheet on the top shelf of the oven to heat up. Line the pastry cases with squares of scrunched-up baking paper large enough to come up the sides, fill with baking beans and bake blind in the oven for 7 minutes. Turn the tray around and bake for another 7 minutes. Remove the beans and paper, brush the bases with the egg white to seal the pastry and bake for a further 2 minutes.

Reduce the oven temperature to 160°C/gas mark 3 and put the shelf lower down in the oven. Crack the eggs into a medium bowl, add the sugar and stir gently using a balloon whisk just to break them up (you don't want to make the mixture frothy), then stir in the lemon juice. Put the cream in a small saucepan, along with the lemon zest. Heat gently until bubbles just start to appear around the sides of the pan. Stirring gently with the whisk, gradually add the hot cream to the egg mixture so the eggs don't scramble.

Put a sieve over a large jug and pour in the lemony mixture. While the pastry is still warm, pour the mixture into the tart cases to about 5mm from the top and very carefully put the tarts in the oven on the lower shelf. Bake for about 15–17 minutes until just set. To avoid overcooking, keep checking every 5 minutes – the second the mixture has only a tiny wobble in the

middle when the tray is moved gently, the tarts are ready.

Take the tins off the tray and place on a wire rack to cool completely. If eating right away, remove from the tins, if keeping for longer than two days, store in their tins in a cool place.

Iced raspberry & coconut ripple

These totally scrumptious flavoured ices are frozen together yet instantly scoopable straight from the freezer. It's so easy to make, the joy being you don't have to rush out and buy an ice cream machine.

enough for 8

For the raspberry sorbet
225g raspberries
75g icing sugar
1 tablespoon lime juice
1 medium egg white

For the coconut ice
300ml coconut milk
4 medium egg yolks
125g caster sugar
1 teaspoon coconut extract
   (optional)
125g pure non-dairy coconut
   yogurt

To make the sorbet, put the raspberries in a pan with 2 tablespoons of the icing sugar and the lime juice. Set over a low heat, stirring to dissolve the sugar and soften the berries, for about 2 minutes. Set a sieve over a bowl, strain the berries and push them through, using the back of a ladle in a circular motion. Discard the seeds. Put the raspberry purée in a small freezerproof container and freeze.

To make the coconut ice, put the coconut milk in a pan and heat gently until bubbles appear around the sides of the pan. Put the egg yolks and sugar into a bowl and whisk until pale and thickened. Pour the hot milk over the yolk mixture and stir. Pour back into the pan and heat, stirring continuously, until the mixture becomes a little thicker (watch the eggs don't scramble; if you have a thermometer, heat to 75°C).

Pour into a bowl and leave until completely cold. Fold through the coconut extract (if using) and the coconut yogurt until evenly mixed. Put in a freezerproof container and freeze overnight. The next day, leave out for 20 minutes until a butter knife cuts through easily and cut the coconut ice into rough cubes in the container, then put the cubes in a food processor and whizz for a few minutes until the mixture has broken down and is completely smooth. Alternatively, churn in an ice-cream machine if you have one, following the manufacturer's instructions.

Put it back into the container and freeze while finishing the sorbet. Remove the berry purée from the freezer and cut into cubes and whizz in the processor in the same way (rinsing it out first).

Whisk the egg white until soft peaks form and add the rest of the icing sugar, a little at a time, whisking continuously. Fold it into the berry purée until it has an even colour. Remove the coconut ice from the freezer (it will still be soft enough), swirl the berry mixture through it and refreeze for a minimum of 5 hours.

Very berry iced soufflés

Make these at the height of summer when the berries are so tasty you can't stop eating them – even better if you can pick your own. If you don't want to mess around making a collar on each ramekin, just fill a few more dishes with the spare mixture, but the added height does make them look lovely, served with some extra fruit on top.

enough for 6

125g strawberries, hulled, plus
  extra to decorate
160g caster sugar
125g raspberries, plus extra to
  decorate
grated zest and juice of ½ lime
4 medium egg whites
pinch of cream of tartar
300ml double cream

Tape a collar of clear acetate (available from art shops, baking shops or online) or baking paper around 6 x 125ml ramekins to come about 2–3cm above the rim.

Finely chop 3 of the strawberries, scatter with a teaspoon of the sugar and set aside. Put the rest of the strawberries and the raspberries in a processor with the lime zest and juice and whizz to a purée.

Put the egg whites and cream of tartar in a large bowl. Use hand-held electric beaters to whisk until firm and the beaters leave a pattern in the mixture. Gradually add the remaining sugar, whisking constantly until stiff and glossy. Without washing the beaters, whisk the cream to the same consistency as the meringue and fold together along with half the berry purée. Fold in the rest of the purée and the finely chopped strawberries.

Pile the mixture into the prepared ramekins to come level with the top of the collar and place on a level shelf in the freezer. Freeze for about 5 hours until firm on top or leave overnight.

When ready to serve, remove the collar and decorate with extra fruit and put in the fridge. The soufflés will be softly scoopable and ready to eat within 10 minutes of taking from the freezer.

baked custard

Prune & custard tarts

Inspired by the Portuguese custard tart, these use prunes –
if they don't appeal, use plump raisins or sultanas or omit
entirely. If you are blessed with patience, take a sharp knife and
cut into the tops of the pastry circles once they are in the tins.
This technique is known as knocking up and helps the layers of
the puff pastry rise separately.

makes 12

80g soft stoned prunes, roughly
  snipped into small pieces
2 teaspoons calvados or brandy
  (optional)
4 medium egg yolks
100g caster sugar, plus a light
  sprinkling for the pastry
400ml full-fat milk
2 tablespoons cornflour
1 tablespoon plain flour
320g all-butter ready, rolled
  puff pastry

Put the prunes in a bowl with the calvados and leave to soak for as long
as possible.

Put the yolks and sugar in a bowl and, using a balloon whisk, mix together
until light and the sugar has dissolved. Add a few spoonfuls of the milk, sift
in the flours and whisk until smooth.

Heat the rest of the milk in a medium pan and gradually whisk into the
egg mixture. Put back into the pan and, over a low–medium heat, stir
constantly with a wooden spoon until you feel it thickening – it will coat the
spoon and leave a thick trail as you stir. Remove from the heat and transfer
to a bowl. Sit the bowl in a basin of cold water to help the custard cool
down quickly. Chill until ready to use.

Unroll the pastry and cut in half across. Sprinkle one half with a little sugar
and place the other half on top. Roll up from the short end as tightly as
possible. Roll backwards and forwards to stretch the log until it measures
30cm. Cut in half and chill for 30 minutes. Cut each piece into 12 and roll
each piece into an 11cm circle with the curl of the roll facing you. Tuck
into the holes of a 12-hole muffin tin, pressing it up to the rim, and chill for
30 minutes.

Preheat the oven to 230°C/gas mark 8.

Mix roughly a third of the custard into the prunes. Spoon this mixture
equally into the pastry cases, then top with the rest of the custard to come
within a little less than 1cm from the top of the pastry. Bake in the oven for
18 minutes until golden. Leave to cool for 5 minutes, remove the tarts from
the tin and put them on a wire rack to cool completely.

batter

Blackberry clafoutis

A classic French clafoutis is a delicious creamy batter affair made with unstoned cherries. My version uses blackberries, but raspberries or a can of drained apricots would also work if you want a quick pudding from the storecupboard. In France, using fruit other than cherries would, strictly speaking, make this a flaugnarde, but let's not go there!

enough for 4

35g butter, melted, plus extra
    for greasing
135g plain flour
75g golden caster sugar
3 large eggs
225ml full-fat milk
450g blackberries
golden icing sugar, for dusting
    (optional)
clotted cream or yogurt, to serve

Preheat the oven to 180° C/gas mark 4. Grease 4 x 250ml shallow gratin dishes with plenty of butter and place on a large baking tray.

Put the dry ingredients in a bowl and make a well in the middle. Crack the eggs into the well and gradually whisk in the milk using a balloon whisk, letting the flour fall gradually into the liquid to avoid lumps. Add the melted butter and whisk to a smooth batter. Pour into a measuring jug (this makes it easier to divide up the batter).

Pour a thin layer of batter into each dish and divide the fruit between them. Pour over the rest of the batter and bake in the oven for 35 minutes until risen and golden. Serve right away, dusted with icing sugar (if using) and accompanied by clotted cream or yogurt.

cake

Chestnut & hazel fudge cake

This cake is based on an old French recipe I rediscovered. In its new glory it is rich in chestnut flavour and colour. Use whole cooked chestnuts to grate over the top to serve. All the ingredients are easy to find in health food shops and some supermarkets.

enough for 8

85g butter, melted, plus extra
    for greasing
100g skinless hazelnuts
25g chestnut flour
150g unsweetened chestnut purée
4 medium eggs
85g date syrup
pinch of cream of tartar

To serve
15g skinless hazelnuts, lightly
    toasted and finely chopped
2 whole cooked chestnuts,
    for grating
50g unsweetened chestnut purée
150ml double cream
1–2 teaspoons date syrup

Preheat the oven to 190°C/gas mark 5. Fully line a greased 20cm springform tin with baking paper.

Finely grind the hazelnuts and chestnut flour together in two batches in a mini processor. Mix the melted butter into the chestnut purée and stir in the hazelnut mixture.

Separate the eggs into two bowls and add roughly half the date syrup to the yolks. Use hand-held electric beaters to whisk the egg whites and cream of tartar together until firm and the beaters leave a pattern in the foam. Gradually add the rest of the date syrup to the egg whites, whisking constantly until glossy.

Without washing the beaters, whisk the egg yolks with date syrup together until thick and creamy. Beat in the chestnut hazel mixture and fold in the egg white mixture, a little at a time, until an even colour. Tip into the tin and bake in the oven for 35 minutes until the middle feels firm to the touch (don't worry if it cracks a little).

Remove from the oven and cool for 10 minutes before removing from the tin and cooling completely on a wire rack.

To serve, scatter with chopped nuts and grate over one of the chestnuts. Whisk the chestnut purée, double cream and date syrup together and serve with the cake. Grate a little extra chestnut over each serving.

baked

Pistachio & chocolate financier

A financier is classically made in small moulds resembling gold bars – hence the name. I have played with it and the result has become one of my favourite ways to use up egg whites without going to a great deal of trouble. The heating of the mixture is crucial as I tried putting in melted butter and the result isn't as good. I love pistachios, but do use all ground almonds if you prefer. You could leave off the spattered chocolate on the top if you don't want it.

makes 12–16 pieces, depending on size

75g butter, cubed, plus extra for greasing
75g pistachio nibs (sliced pistachios)
120g caster sugar
1½ tablespoons plain flour
25g ground almonds
4 medium egg whites
35g dark chocolate (70 per cent cocoa solids; optional)

Preheat the oven to 190°C/gas mark 5. Grease the base and sides of a 17cm square tin with sides 3cm deep, then line the base with baking paper. Grind the pistachios, half the sugar and the flour in batches in a coffee grinder or a mini processor until very finely ground.

Put the butter cubes into a medium pan with the rest of the sugar. Add the ground pistachio mixture along with the ground almonds. Mix in the egg whites and use a wooden spoon to stir furiously and continuously over a low heat until all the cubes of butter have melted and the mixture has come together in a creamy mass. (It takes only about 2 minutes to melt the butter, so don't stop stirring and don't abandon it or it will overheat.) Tip into the prepared tin and bake in the oven for 20–25 minutes until pale golden and firm to a gentle touch.

Leave to cool for 3 minutes. Tip the cake out onto a baking tray lined with a sheet of baking paper. Peel off the lining paper, then swiftly invert it onto a wire rack so that it is the right way up and leave to cool completely. Cut into as many pieces as you like with a serrated bread knife but don't separate the pieces out until you add the chocolate.

Break the chocolate into a heatproof bowl and set it over a smaller pan of simmering water so that the base doesn't come into contact with the water. Melt for 4 minutes, then remove the bowl and stir until completely melted. Leave to cool for 5 minutes. Using a pointed teaspoon (or a piping bag made by folding baking paper into a cone and snipping off the end after filling), splatter the top of the cake with the chocolate and leave it to set hard.

baked

Bread, caramel & peanut butter pudding with nectarines

Maybe a bit of an indulgence, but this is divine with clotted cream and just as good with yogurt. If you can leave it until cold, it's perfect – or let it sit for 30 minutes or so before serving. Use dulce de leche or look for a can of 'caramel to cook with', which is usually next to the condensed milk in the supermarket.

enough for 6–8

3 large eggs
125g dulce de leche from a jar
40g demerara sugar, plus extra
   for dusting
300ml double cream
50ml full-fat milk
250g good-quality bread, cut into
   1.75cm slices
100g smooth peanut butter
2 nectarines, cut into wedges

Have ready a 1-litre capacity (about 22 x 16cm) ovenproof gratin dish with sides around 5cm deep. Crack the eggs into a large bowl and use a balloon whisk to mix in 2 tablespoons of the dulce de leche and all the sugar. Add the cream and milk and whisk until smooth.

Spread the peanut butter onto half the bread slices, followed by the rest of the dulce de leche on top of the peanut butter, then sandwich together with the remaining bread slices. Cut each sandwich into 4, roughly the shape of a triangle, and arrange in the gratin dish with the point uppermost. Pour over the egg mixture, insert the wedges of nectarine and scatter with a little extra demerara sugar. Leave to soak for 5 minutes.

Preheat the oven to 160°C/gas mark 3. Put the dish in a deep roasting tin and pour in hot water from a boiled kettle to come half-way up the sides of the dish. Bake in the oven for 30 minutes or until just set. Take out of the roasting tin and leave for about 15 minutes before serving warm or longer to serve cold.

custard & meringue

Tropical îles flottantes

I like the flavour of coconut sugar, but it's quite chunky and has a high water content, which isn't so easy for meringue-making. So I make this work by drying it in the oven, then whizz it to a fine powder using a coffee grinder. You could make the custard and mango sauce in advance and keep in the fridge.

enough for 6–8

425g can mango slices, drained, or 3 Alphonso or other ripe mangoes, peeled, stoned and sliced
juice of ½ small lime
85g organic coconut sugar
2 medium egg whites
½ teaspoon cream of tartar

For the custard
400ml organic coconut milk
3 medium eggs
2 medium egg yolks
5 tablespoons caster sugar
½ teaspoon coconut extract (optional)

To make the custard, put the coconut milk in a medium saucepan and bring to a simmer. Meanwhile, whisk together the eggs, yolks, sugar and coconut extract in a bowl, then gradually stir in the hot coconut milk. Pour back into the pan and put over the lowest heat. Stir continuously with a balloon whisk for about 2 minutes until it thickens a little. Make sure it gets no hotter than 80°C or the eggs will curdle. It thickens up a lot as it cools. Strain into a bowl and put the base into a bigger bowl of cold water to stop the cooking.

Whizz the mango slices to a purée in a mini processor. Push through a sieve using the back of a ladle and discard the bits left behind. Stir in the lime juice and set aside while you make the meringues.

Spread the coconut sugar on a tray lined with baking paper and put in the oven at 110°C/gas mark ¼. Leave to heat and dry for 20 minutes. Tip into a coffee grinder and whizz to a fine powder.

When ready to serve, fill a large (shallow if possible) pan with boiling water and set over a low heat.

Put a double layer of kitchen paper on the work surface. Put the egg whites and cream of tartar in a large bowl. Use hand-held electric beaters to whisk until firm and the beaters leave a pattern in the mixture. Gradually add half the powdered coconut sugar, whisking constantly to a stiff meringue. Using a large metal spoon, gently fold in the rest of the sugar, keeping the volume.

Quickly pour the custard into shallow serving bowls. Scoop up teaspoonfuls of the meringue and gently place on the surface of the hot water. Cook about six at a time for about 1 minute. Lift out each one with a slotted spoon, letting its base drain on kitchen paper for a second, then slide onto the custard. Spoon over the mango sauce and serve right away.

souffléd

Easy orange soufflés

A delicious end to a meal, lavish yet so simple to have at the
ready. Butter the ramekins or soufflé dishes and sit them on a
baking tray in the fridge to get ahead. Once the mixture is in the
ramekins they can be kept in the fridge while you eat your main
course – just make sure you have the oven nice and hot.

enough for 8

butter, for greasing
325g jar of orange curd
finely grated zest of 1 small
    orange
2 tablespoons curaçao
6 large egg whites
pinch of cream of tartar
50g caster sugar
icing sugar, sifted, for dusting

Butter 8 x 150ml ramekins or heatproof dishes generously and put on an
oven tray in the fridge for at least 15 minutes.

Preheat the oven to 200°C/gas mark 6. Put the orange curd and orange
zest in a small pan and warm through over a low heat for 1 minute, remove
from the heat and add the curaçao. Transfer to a large bowl.

Put the egg whites and cream of tartar in a medium bowl. Use hand-held
electric beaters to whisk until firm and the beaters leave a pattern in the
foam. Gradually add the sugar, whisking constantly to a glossy meringue.

Use a metal spoon to fold the meringue mixture carefully into the curd
mixture until an even colour. Spoon into the buttered ramekins and smooth
the tops with a spatula. Run a thumb around the inside of the rim of each
ramekin to separate the mixture from the edge – this helps to give an even
rise. You can put them back in the fridge at this point for 30 minutes.

Bake in the oven for 12 minutes until risen and golden on top. Dust with the
icing sugar and serve right away.

under the grill

Strawberries & peach schnapps sabayon

The simplest of desserts, making it a great finish to a meal with friends. Strawberries taste best at room temperature, so buy them ripe, keep in a paper bag and use them within a few days.

enough for 4

14–18 strawberries, hulled and
  halved
½ teaspoon vanilla sugar

For the peach schnapps sabayon
3 large egg yolks
2 tablespoons caster sugar
2 tablespoons peach schnapps

Mix the strawberries with the sugar and leave to macerate.

To make the sabayon, put the yolks, sugar and schnapps in a medium heatproof bowl. Use hand-held electric beaters to whisk together until pale, then set the bowl over a pan of gently simmering water so the base doesn't touch the water.

Whisk for about 5 minutes until thick, pale and you can see the bottom of the bowl as you whisk. Remove from the pan and continue to whisk for a few minutes until thick and just warm.

Preheat the grill to high and put the shelf in the middle of the oven. Drain the strawberries and divide between four shallow gratin dishes or one large one and place on an oven tray. Spoon over the sabayon and grill for a few seconds – only until golden (keep a very close eye on them as the tops burn very fast). Eat right away.

batter

Dutch puffs

Also known as a Dutch baby or German oven pancakes. I like to serve these with scoops of Pecan praline semifreddo (see page 200). Small tin plates or shallow ovenproof gratin dishes are ideal for them or make one large puff in a frying pan or roasting tin for sharing.

enough for 4

150g plain flour
1 tablespoon caster sugar, plus a little extra for dusting the tins
3 large eggs
250ml full-fat milk
1 teaspoon vanilla essence
small knobs of butter for the plates/dishes
pinch of sea salt crystals
Pecan praline semifreddo (see page 200) or any bought ice cream, to serve

Sift the flour into a medium bowl and make a well in the middle. Whisk the sugar, eggs, milk, vanilla and salt together. Pour about quarter of the mixture into the flour and whisk using electric hand-held beaters, letting the flour fall naturally into the liquid (this avoids lumps). As the mixture thickens add more liquid until all the flour falls in and all the liquid is used up. Rest the batter for 30 minutes–1 hour.

Meanwhile, preheat the oven to 220°/gas mark 7.

Put 4 x 12.5cm diameter small pans, tin plates or gratin dishes with sides 2–3cm deep in the oven to heat up for 5 minutes. Add the butter and heat in the oven for a minute. Ladle in the batter to come 1½cm from the top of the containter and bake for about 18–20 minutes until puffed and golden.

Scoop some Pecan praline semifreddo onto each one and serve while hot so it melts a little.

in the freezer

Pecan praline semifreddo

You could use any nut you like for this. The recipe makes plenty to serve on its own with enough for another time used as a topping for the Dutch Puffs (see page 198). Add a flurry of the excess praline to the top of your ice-cream scoops.

enough for a crowd

6 medium egg yolks
125ml maple syrup
250g mascarpone
150ml double cream

For the praline
3 tablespoons water
100g golden caster sugar
20g butter, cubed
150g pecan nuts, roughly chopped

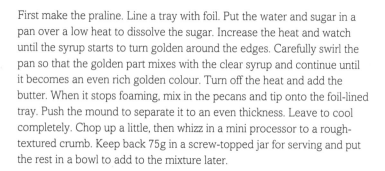

First make the praline. Line a tray with foil. Put the water and sugar in a pan over a low heat to dissolve the sugar. Increase the heat and watch until the syrup starts to turn golden around the edges. Carefully swirl the pan so that the golden part mixes with the clear syrup and continue until it becomes an even rich golden colour. Turn off the heat and add the butter. When it stops foaming, mix in the pecans and tip onto the foil-lined tray. Push the mound to separate it to an even thickness. Leave to cool completely. Chop up a little, then whizz in a mini processor to a rough-textured crumb. Keep back 75g in a screw-topped jar for serving and put the rest in a bowl to add to the mixture later.

Use hand-held electric beaters to whisk the egg yolks and maple syrup in a large heatproof bowl until paler in colour. Set the bowl over a pan of barely simmering water, making sure the bowl doesn't touch the water, and whisk until the mixture doubles in volume. Remove the bowl, put in a larger bowl of cold water and continue to whisk until cool. Leave to chill for 10 minutes.

Put the marcarpone in a bowl and mix in the cream. Add a little of the cold egg mixture to loosen it, then gently fold in the rest. Fold in the praline and transfer to a freezerproof container. Freeze for about 9 hours until firm, or overnight. Serve scattered with some of the praline stored in the jar.

Chocolate & salted caramel mousse

If you think you can't use so many, simply halve the ingredients to make 4. Small cups, glasses or ramekins are fine to use – make sure they are around 125ml capacity.

enough for 8

250g dark chocolate (85% cocoa solids)
5 tablespoons salted caramel sauce or dulce de leche with a pinch of sea salt added, both shop-bought
4 medium eggs
pinch of cream of tartar
2 tablespoons organic coconut sugar or golden caster sugar
150ml double cream

Break the chocolate into a large heatproof bowl, add the salted caramel sauce and set it over a smaller pan of simmering water so that the base of the bowl doesn't come into contact with the water. Melt for 5 minutes, then remove the bowl and stir until completely melted. Pour into a medium bowl and set aside for 5 minutes.

Separate the eggs, putting the whites in a medium bowl with the cream of tartar and the yolks in a small one. Whisk the whites to soft peaks, until the beaters leave a pattern in the foam, and gradually add the sugar, whisking between each addition. Without washing the beaters, whip the cream until floppy.

Mix the egg yolks into the chocolate mixture (don't worry if it stiffens) and mix in the whipped cream. Fold in the whisked egg white mixture until an even colour and spoon into 125ml containers. Put on a tray and chill for a minimum of 5 hours or overnight. They will keep for three days in the fridge.

Orange & soft goat's cheese crespelle

Like crêpes suzette, Italian crespelle are folded, except these are first filled with an orange-zesty and salty-sharp cream cheese, then bathed in orange sauce before serving. Make the crespelle the day before if you want and store them flat in an airtight container in a cool place. Briefly warm before fillling, folding and immersing.

makes 12 crespelle – enough for 4–6

4–5 large oranges, finely zested
   then juiced (you need 300ml
   freshly squeezed juice)
70g golden caster sugar
150g soft goat's cheese
85g butter
115g plain flour
3 large eggs
pinch of cream of tartar
275ml milk
2 teaspoons pure orange essence
   (optional)

Mix the orange zest with 1 tablespoon of the sugar and mix a teaspoon of it into the goat's cheese and set aside. Put the orange juice and 2 tablespoons of the sugar in a medium pan over a low heat and, when the sugar dissolves, increase the heat and bring to a simmer. Reduce to around 175ml and mix in 25g of the butter. Set aside and keep warm.

Put the flour and 1 tablespoon of the sugar in a medium bowl and make a well in the middle. Separate one of the eggs, putting the white in a large bowl with the cream of tartar and the yolk in with the flour. Crack the other eggs into the flour and add the milk and orange essence (if using).

Using hand-held electric beaters, whisk the white until the beaters leave a pattern in the foam, then whisk in the rest of the sugar, a little at a time, until stiff. Without washing the beaters, whisk the batter mixture, allowing the flour to fall naturally into the liquid (this avoids lumps). Gradually and gently fold the batter into the whisked white using a metal spoon.

Heat a knob of the butter in a 20–22cm-base frying pan over a medium heat and swirl the pan to coat evenly. Pour in a 45ml ladleful of batter and swirl around the pan until it coats the base evenly. After about 1½ minutes, flip the crespelle over and cook the other side for 30 seconds. Tip onto a board so the underside is uppermost. Form a pile of crespelle as you cook the rest in the same way.

When all are cooked, spread a few knobs of the goat's cheese mixture on one half of each crespelle and fold in quarters. Put three at a time back into the frying pan, add some of the orange sauce and heat to warm them. As they heat, lay them in a large dish. There will be orange sauce left in the pan, so add any butter left from cooking the crespelle, simmer for a minute to a syrupy glaze and pour over them. Serve on plates sprinkled with the sugary orange zest.

Index

Acknowledgements

A huge than...   ...y to crack

to the many

who helped

generously i...   ...eping me from

making of th...   ...company

without then

not have bee...   ...s for the job and

...e bit.

...Abramovich for
...y things.

...r happy garden

Finally, the inspiration behind Cracked, is strangely enough, the chef Marcel
Boulestin for his book written on eggs in 1932. I bought it a few years ago,
seduced by the cover, from a dusty shelf in a second-hand book shop and vowed
I would one day write this book…

Suppliers

Good assorted eggs of all types with seasonal availability
www.clarencecourt.co.uk
Bantam and coloured eggs - Rainbow Eggs www.therainboweggcompany.co.uk
For egg information from the Soil Association www.soilassociation.org
Hard to find ingredients www.souschef.co.uk
Blackacre Farm for free range duck eggs –
www.thetraditionalfreerangeeggcompany.co.uk
Duck egg blue electric hand whisks – Candy Rose collection www.dunelm.com
For beetroot powder – wholefoods – www.wholefoodsmarket.com